Aspects of modern sociology

Social research

Book

GENERAL EDITORS

John Barron Mays
Eleanor Rathbone Professor of Sociology, University of Liverpool

Maurice Craft
Senior Lecturer in Education, University of Exeter

Deciphering Data

The analysis of social surveys

Jonathan Silvey

Lecturer in Applied Social Science
University of Nottingham

CHESTER COLLEGE	
ACC. No. 75/2431	DEPT.
CLASS No. 301,0723 SIL	
LIBRARY	

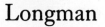

Longman

LONGMAN GROUP LIMITED
London
and LONGMAN INC., New York
*Associated companies, branches and representatives
throughout the world*

© Longman Group Limited 1975

All rights reserved. No part of this publication may be reproduced, stored in a
retrieval system, or transmitted in any form or by any means, electronic,
mechanical, photocopying, recording, or otherwise, without the prior permission
of the Copyright owner.

First published 1975

ISBN 0582 48040 X cased
            48041 8 paper
Library of Congress Catalog Card Number 74–76123

*Computer Typesetting by
Print Origination Bootle, Lancs L20 6NS*

*and printed in Great Britain by
Lowe & Brydone (Printers) Ltd, Thetford, Norfolk*

Contents

Acknowledgements

We are grateful to the following for permission to reproduce copyright material:

American Sociological Association for 'Hired Hand Research' by J. Roth in *American Sociologist,* 1; The Controller of Her Majesty's Stationery Office for tables adapted from *'Road Accidents'* 1970 H.M.S.O. 1972, 'Children and their Primary Schools' in *Plowden Report 1967, Vol. 2, Appendix 3* and Macmillan Publishing Co. Inc., for a table adapted from *'The Language of Social Research'* 1955 by P.F. Lazarfeld & M. Rosenberg.

We regret that we have been unable to trace Dataset Ltd., to whom we are indebted for the figure of an interpreted, 80 column, punched card.

Editors' Preface

The first series in Longman's *Aspects of Modern Sociology* library was concerned with the social structure of modern Britain, and was intended for students following professional and other courses in universities, polytechnics, colleges of education, and elsewhere in further and higher education, as well as for those members of a wider public wishing to pursue an interest in the nature and structure of British society.

This further series sets out to examine the history, aims, techniques and limitations of social research, and it is hoped that it will be of interest to the same readership. It will seek to offer an informative but not uncritical introduction to some of the methodologies of social science.

JOHN BARRON MAYS
MAURICE CRAFT

Foreword

This book discusses the final stages in the life history of a social survey, the analysis and interpretation of the data collected. It is a convenient fiction to isolate this phase from the process of survey design and data collection; in reality, analysis and interpretation cannot be satisfactorily achieved when divorced from an intimate understanding of the aims of the designers, the procedures of the interviewers and, we will insist, some prior knowledge of the respondent population. Nor is analysis the purely mechanical process which hiving it off for separate treatment may imply. In justification we plead the need to restore the balance in discussions of survey procedures: the average text gives but a cursory nod towards analysis, as though further explication is unnecessary. As a result, or perhaps as cause, many survey reports present only a fraction of the ore which could be extracted, contenting themselves with a series of tables each showing the relations between two variables. Such approaches harm social science: they leave the impression of regularities in social life which further analysis might explain away, or show to be more distant links in a chain, or show to hold only in certain circumstances. Some of the techniques for investigating these possibilities are simple matters of resorting the data; others involve more sophisticated analysis. In both categories we hope to enable the reader to understand the results, and in the former to undertake such analyses when the opportunity arises.

We have tried to set survey analysis and the social survey, as tools of social research, into both logical and theoretical perspectives. Techniques are dealt with, but we hope by setting them in this larger context to stimulate the inquirer to see the substantive and methodological possibilities and limits of the social survey. With the advent of computers to data-processing, a much wider variety of analytic techniques become a practical proposition. Their results, unlike percentages but necessarily numerical, cannot be translated easily into a literary form. To do so, indeed, would often distort the reality and complexity of the data. It is no longer the case that the methods available produce results which happen to fit the needs of an innumerate readership. To gain the maximum benefit with the minimum of distortion, these more recent developments presuppose a high quality of data. Leaving aside the methods of data-collection, which are important but beyond the scope of this book, the quality of data can all too easily be reduced in the process of classification, and in the calculation of summary statistics. In chapter 2, we discuss classifying practices and the choice of statistics appropriate to the data-as-classified. Chapter 3 considers how to produce tables, the traditional and the most readily comprehensible way of presenting results, and introduces the reader to using computers for survey analysis. This chapter will be 'old hat' to those not new to the game.

With chapters 4 and 5, we turn from the 'recipe-book' approach to discuss ways of making sense of a data-set, focussing on how we might tease out plausible cause-and-effect relationships. These chapters contain introductory accounts of the techniques of multiple regression, factor analysis, path analysis and the detection of interaction effects.

Before embarking upon how social surveys can be analysed, we should consider their nature in the social context of the knowledge industries, and how they have developed to date. This is the subject of the first chapter.

I wish to thank Gill Pascall, Philip Bean, Ken Levine and Sy Yasin for their helpful comments on some or all the manuscript; they are not responsible for the errors and infelicities which remain. My wife, Janta, has helped at all stages with her support and eagerness to see it finished. Maurice Craft displayed great patience as an editor. Janet Worthy and Mrs. Ruth Robinson typed the first and final drafts.

JONATHAN SILVEY

The nature of survey analysis   1

Few books on social survey methods offer much advice on data analysis. Their authors tend to devote most attention to the more rigorous procedures used in social surveys, the processes of survey design, sampling and statistical tests of the results, together with hints on questionnaire design, the order and wording of questions, interviewing, and the process of producing tables of results. There is much less discussion of the analysis procedures which lead to a coherent picture of the survey data. Nor do actual survey reports help much. The tables and statistics as published are almost certainly only a selection of those produced in preparing the report. They constitute only a small fraction of the procedures which could have been carried out.

There are at least two reasons for this neglect. Textbooks on methods assume that the surveyor knows exactly what he wants to find out about the population he investigates. The choice of population, the selection of topics to investigate, the construction of the questions themselves, the pilot studies preceding the main survey and the pre-testing of questionnaires, all these stages make little sense unless the surveyor knows precisely what his objectives are in undertaking a survey. Once the objectives are clear and the tactical decisions are made, the appropriate analytical steps are assumed to be predetermined. In effect, these texts say, 'Given enough foresight, who needs hindsight?'

In practice, however, any survey will pose more questions in the mind of the researcher than it answers. Clues to some of these questions may be available in the data already collected. If he is to take advantage of them, unforeseen methods of analysis will have to be used. Imagination and ingenuity, for which no textbook can provide a blueprint, are necessary. Such qualities can be facilitated by the experience of other analysts if formulated into guide lines, but they cannot be prescribed as a recipe or set of rules.

Secondly, a survey can sometimes be an early step in opening up a new field of inquiry. In this case, the variables most relevant in this new field are the result of inspired guesswork or are derived from current theory. It is for the survey data itself to demonstrate the relevance or otherwise of these hunches. The primary objective of this type of survey is to clarify the incidence of certain features in a population. These surveys are called *descriptive* because they describe some facets of social life. Sometimes so little may be known either about the basic facts of a new area of inquiry or about the feasibility of making an investigation that an initial *pilot* or *feasibility* survey has to be followed up by a larger scale descriptive survey, the items of which have been decided on in the light of the earlier results. A descriptive study requires, for the finished product, statements and tables showing how respondents vary in their answer to each question, and sometimes the degree of association between the more important variables and the basic demographic variables such as age and sex. Non-routine analysis begins when these *marginal distributions* (the straight frequency counts) and *relationships* prompt the question, 'Why?'

Suppose for example, one was investigating the ways in which adolescents took up, or avoided, habitual smoking, in the hope that this knowledge could be used to discourage taking up smoking more effectively. Common knowledge would suggest that adolescence, or some period in it, is critical for future smoking habits. If a youngster avoids smoking then, he is much less likely to take it up later; conversely, if he has developed a liking or need for cigarettes in his youth, he is more prone to continue later.

A social researcher starting this inquiry would need more specific information than this. Can there be said to be a critical risk period for most adolescents? At what ages does it occur? Does it differ for boys and girls, or for different social backgrounds, or different school-leaving ages? How many people smoke by the age of, say twenty, and how committed to it are they then? The investigator might decide that the core of his research will be a survey of samples of school pupils in the main risk groups, to discover what kinds of attitudes and social backgrounds distinguish smokers from non-smokers. When a survey demonstrates the kinds of factors distinguishing different types of behaviour, it is called *explanatory* because, in some sense, the behaviour is explained by being shown to depend upon differences in earlier factors. But before he can undertake this hypothesis-testing stage, the researcher must know a great deal more about the field (descriptive surveys) and, indeed, whether he is likely to get valid information about smoking, attitudes, and social backgrounds from the critical groups in the way he proposes (feasibility or pilot studies). The explanatory survey will be only as good as the hypotheses tested allow. If they are naive or fallacious, little is likely to result from the explanatory survey. One of the main sources of imaginative and precise hypotheses will be the analyses and interpretations he makes of previous surveys.

ARE SURVEYS OBJECTIVE?

It is often said that one of the canons of the scientific method is replicability. This means that the reader of a scientific report is told so precisely how an experiment has been carried out, and with what results, that he could repeat or *replicate* the procedure and determine whether he obtains the same results. If the results are verified, the only difference between the two reports may be in their interpretation. In this way scientific knowledge is self-correcting because unlikely findings can be checked and rechecked. Knowledge is objective, in this view, to the extent that different observers, preferably with varying preconceptions, arrive at the same conclusions about the 'facts' when using the same methods of inquiry. The derived facts are thus independent of the observer's preconceptions. The same knowledge lies in the minds of all the beholders.

Most people would probably assume that, in theory at least, the sample survey is a technique for obtaining a comparable level of objective knowledge. A good survey report spells out its methods in detail, questionnaires are reproduced verbatim, and statistical tests are used to calculate both significant departures from those expected from random sampling and the degree of accuracy to be attached to sample estimates of population characteristics. In other words, even if no one

3

else can ever actually repeat the same survey at the same point in time with the same interviewers, enough detail is given to enable an experienced survey reader to repeat in his imagination the methods used. Standardised methods of obtaining information from respondents, using the same script for all interviewers, is a defining characteristic of a social survey because the main features of the methods used are readily communicable to others. At the least, then, experienced survey practitioners can evaluate a survey report and judge the extent to which the results should be taken seriously. Surveys are subject to the criterion of *imaginative replicability,* the extent to which the procedures used are public knowledge, and can be mentally recapitulated by those with the experience to judge.

Notice, however, some rather crucial differences between this kind of objective knowledge and that obtained by repeated experiments. Survey procedures, in common with all social science techniques, can never be exactly repeated because if the same individuals were to be studied, the repetition itself might affect their attitudes and behaviour, and if other, randomly selected individuals formed the sample, events and experiences since the time of the earlier survey may have reduced the comparability of the new subjects. Thus marginally different results do not necessarily cast doubt on the 'objectivity' of an earlier survey to the same degree that they would a replicated experiment with inanimate materials.

These objections to the objective status of social surveys may be thought somewhat unrealistic, since in practice surveys rarely inquire into ephemeral attitudes or patterns of behaviour. With the exception of pre-election opinion polls, where attention is directed towards fluctuations in voting intentions, most surveys are concerned with deeper rooted, less variable, factors. They could be replicated on a comparable group—another sample of the same population perhaps—and within the normal limits of sampling variability, comparable results should be obtained.

Only up to a point, for although the data collected and available to the survey analysts may be comparable, their reports and interpretations of the data will differ. Whenever survey reports go beyond the specific objectives with which they started, objectives

4

which indeed are so specific that they really constitute a set of instructions for analysis procedures, different authors will use different methods of analysis to reach their conclusions. Most experienced social researchers find that in practice data tends to be 'robust', that is to produce the same kind of answers whether one uses highly sophisticated procedures or a shortcut route, violating many assumptions about the data.

At the level of data validity, Lazarsfeld calls this effect the 'interchangeability of indices', and reminds us that this implies that 'we can never reach "pure class" classifications. Whatever index we use, the items will have "peculiarities" which result in some cases being misclassified, and therefore the empirical relationships which we find are lower than they would be if we had more precise measures of the variables with which the study is concerned'.[1]

The same may be said of statistical shortcuts. It is quite common to find data stretched beyond its proper limits in statistical analyses. We discuss some of these limits in the next chapter; the point here is that experience is often that the data tells essentially the same tale despite the methodological violence done to it. Since interpretations of social data are usually couched in terms of one variable, X_a, being more (or less) closely associated with another, Y, than is a third, X_b, the absolute magnitude of a statistic is of less importance than its size relative to other statistics obtained. In other words, conclusions based on sophisticated calculations and assumptions tend to be expressed in literary form as though they were less sophisticated kinds of measurements. Thus, despite the illegitimate procedures, the interpreted results are the same as would have occurred with less convenient methods of analysis. Recently social scientists have more openly expressed their dissatisfaction with this innumerate approach to the reporting of findings. We take up this theme in the final chapter.

SURVEY ANALYSIS AS A CRAFT

Survey analysis also permits a variety of routes to the same end, the 'explanation' of some factors in terms of others. An experiment at the Survey Research Centre of the University of California illustrates the unmechanical nature of analysis.[2] Three highly experienced investigators, all graduates of Columbia University's Bureau of Applied Social Research and all teaching the same methodology course at Berkeley, analysed independently the same data. They were instructed to trace the sources of support for communism or capitalism using data from a sample of young Italian men.

In the experiment each one was instructed to analyse survey data from a sample of young Italian men in order to determine what led some to support capitalism and others communism. Each was provided with a team of statisticians so that he could rapidly obtain whatever sets of percentaged tables he required. As he worked through the analysis, each tape-recorded his comments while another experienced researcher, acting as interviewer-observer, ensured that as each table was scanned the investigator recorded what he saw in it and what lines of approach it suggested to him. At the end of the day, each investigator drafted a report on what he had done and what he would have done, given more time.

As Hirschi and Selvin say, if 'social research is really the mechanical process that has been claimed, then surely there was every reason to expect these three . . . to turn out a standard, assembly-line product'. As they were all using the same data it is hardly surprising that they all reached the same conclusions. 'What was totally unexpected, and is particularly impressive in view of their similar backgrounds, is that all three followed significantly different plans of analysis', and the divergences would have been even greater had there been more time.[3] Social survey analysis is, then, a craft and the final product will reflect the skills of the craftsman as well as the 'facts of the case'. No two products will be identical.

IMPLICIT UNDERSTANDING BETWEEN RESPONDENTS, REPORT ANALYST AND READER

It is important to notice that a survey report is basically for 'home consumption only'. Analyst, audience and respondents need to share many basic assumptions if the reader is to 'understand' the behaviour and attitudes of the aggregated respondents, as these are presented to him by the analytic report writer. If a European or American were reading the results of a survey of the nutritional habits of an African pastoralist community, what would he make of the finding that, say, 'the great majority said their favourite meal was a souffléd mixture of cow's blood and milk, while 2 per cent (all males) chose egg-based dishes'? He would either have to know beforehand, or the analyst must spell it out, that cattle are the only stable source of food available, that poultry is rarely kept, and that there is a taboo against women eating eggs.[4] Without this contextual knowledge, the reader can only have one of two reactions: if the finding bores him, he may feel prompted to retort, 'So what?', and if it interests him it is likely to be stored in his memory in a 'believe it or not', useless information, category. In neither case does the information enlarge his understanding of the community in question.

Unless, therefore, the reader shares (or the analyst communicates to him) what the respondents take for granted, he cannot easily comprehend the views and behaviour which the survey reports. This is not the place to get involved in the developing world of ethnomethodology associated with Garfinkel, Cicourel and others, but their approach has two implications for social surveys. First, the survey is most appropriately used when respondents, interviewers, survey analysts, and readership all share or can comprehend a basic set of assumptions. It is not an appropriate tool for the investigation of exotic or highly deviant groups; here the anthropologist's tools are more appropriate. It is a tool for differentiating among sub-groups of a social collectivity based upon a common denominator of values and assumptions about everyday life.

Mediating between the respondents' answers and the readers' awareness of them is the survey analyst, with his own values, theoretical orientation and personal experience of the respondents' definition of the situation. All these are ingredients making up what Sjoberg has called the 'contextual basis for interpreting findings'.

The author once undertook to write up the results of a survey of police officers arresting for drunkenness. By collecting more detailed information about each offence that can be gained from brief court appearances, the aim was to clarify the reasons for variations in drunkenness conviction rates in different areas. The attempt was not very successful, partly because the data consisted only of those cases where the police had made an arrest, thus excluding those where they had used their discretion and not arrested, but partly because the analyst lacked a background knowledge of police procedures and of the practical implications of a force changing from a beat system to panda car patrols.

We may distinguish between two kinds of contexts.* The African and the police examples illustrate problems which can arise from a lack of familiarity with the macro-context. Without an understanding of the structures of procedures of these two sub-cultures, it is difficult to interpret the significance of the distributions of replies, and their interrelationships.

More serious than these relatively rare macro-contextual problems are those arising from the micro-context. Here, it is the meaning of individual verbal replies which become problematic, when we consider the variety of respondents' personal biographies and situations. Our concern is not so much with the odd individual with a unique misunderstanding of the researcher's intentions, but with larger groups of respondents who give an unintended meaning to questions. The meaning of their responses is equally likely to elude or mislead the analyst.

In other words, quantitative data (the facts) do not speak for themselves; they demand to be set in a qualitative background, which itself is only known to the author or reader from their personal experience. As Sjoberg puts it:

> Sociologists are often unaware of the critical role of case materials for interpreting numerical data [because] they tend to carry out research only within their own society.... When [they] study cultures divergent from their own, they become more aware of the role of the case materials, whether normal, deviant, or extreme in the interpretation of tabular data.[5]

Second, akin to the role of contextual knowledge in understanding numerical results, are the presuppositions of the survey designer and

* I am indebted to Ken Levine for making this distinction.

analyst. From whatever sources they are derived, whether wide-ranging pilot studies, intuitive hunches, conventional wisdom, meticulous previous investigations or a developed theory, both the choice of variables and the way in which they are subsequently analysed reflect the particular perspective of the analyst. Little is usually gained from a survey in which the questions were inserted for no purpose, other than a vague hunch that 'it might be interesting'. As before, results based on such questions are likely to elicit 'So what?' reactions. Like all sociology, surveys are inevitably written from a selective perspective which informs the interpretation of the data. The analyst must, therefore, in fairness to his readers, consciously recognise his particular interpretative stance and make explicit the theory which determines his analysis (an exercise which can be guaranteed to improve the analysis). The claim to 'let the facts speak for themselves' is nonsense; they demand an interpreter.

As an example of the way in which personal experience of the subject matter of a survey and ideological preferences can influence the presentation of a report, we need to go no further than one of the best known British studies, *Family and Kinship in East London*, recently reappraised by Platt.[6] A representative sample survey of 933 adults in Bethnal Green was interviewed and a subsample, all married and with two children under fifteen, was drawn from the larger survey for intensive interviews. Platt points out that the authors themselves only interviewed the latter group, and that they appear to read into the statistical results from the representative sample what they have learnt by direct contact to be true of the unrepresentative marriage sample. 'It is hard to avoid the feeling that the researchers themselves have been carried away by the human qualities of their data on the marriage sample ... [which] is heavily used for the general description of the community.'[7]

The bulk of the material presented consists of quotations illustrating the frequency counts. The function of such material is normally to provide an understanding of the numerical information, first to the authors and then to the reader. But here

the usual procedure of illustrating the hard data with examples is reversed: the anecodotes are illustrated by occasional figures. But the figures only 'illustrate' the anecdotes in a limited sense since they are not on precisely the same subject; in this . . . instance, they tell nothing about the context of the interaction [between mothers and daughters] , only its frequency. They cannot tell anything about content since no questions have been put to the general sample on it.[8]

In other words, Young and Wilmott have deprived both themselves as interpreters of the data, and consequently their readers, of a method of understanding the substance behind the figures. Their understanding may have been correct; in the absence of a representative cross-section of quotations from the general sample we have no way of telling. In this respect, *Family and Kinship in East London* fails to meet the demands of imaginative replicability which we have seen is an important safeguard of a survey's objectivity.

Singling out Young and Wilmott's first work does not mean that it demands critical evaluation more than other well-known studies. It is much easier to be a good armchair critic than a competent practitioner. In an influential article, Deming has classified thirteen major sources of potential errors affecting the ultimate usefulness of a survey.[9] Each factor covers a broad spectrum of possibilities, and a decision to reduce the effect of one kind of error may well increase the likelihood of other types occurring. A research plan is, at best, a considered and calculated set of compromises based on the aims of research, the resources available, and the social realities of the field of investigation. Ideally only the first should determine the research procedures. Much can be learnt by re-examining the methods of influential and significant studies conducted by the most expert practitioners. In the United States, where major advances in research methods have come from such reappraisals, the critics have been practitioners as distinguished as the authors under examination.

BRITISH AND AMERICAN CONTRIBUTIONS TO THE DEVELOPMENT OF SURVEYS

Sadly, in Britain, we have no such tradition even though crucial aspects of social surveys were pioneered here. They were mainly in methods of data collection and in demonstrating the power and utility of statistical descriptions of populations and social problems. John Gaunt (1620-74) first studied the regularities in life spans, and related birth and death rates to occupations. Halley (of Halley's Comet fame) published the first mortality tables in the eighteenth century; their actuarial approach influenced the early nineteenth-century London and Manchester Statistical Societies. These in turn demonstrated enthusiastically the wealth of useful information to be gained from counting and summarising the varieties of social conditions of the day. In this climate of opinion, government departments were required to publish accounts, not only of their financial expenditure, but also of the frequency of their different activities, in the form of Official Statistics. At the end of the century, William Booth in East London, and Rowntree in York demonstrated the potential of the social survey as a tool of social welfare description by their methods of intensive, 'wholesale interviewing' as one of Booth's assistants, later Beatrice Webb, described it. While Francis Galton, Karl Pearson, William Yule and R. A. Fisher were laying the foundations for a science of statistics, Bowley in the early twentieth century developed the *sample* social survey in his study of five English towns.

These British contributions to the developments of the social survey are characterised by an emphasis on the more definite and tangible aspects of surveys: problems of sampling respondents, estimating the characteristics of populations with specified degrees of certainty, quantifying relationships in the data. Even the data collected has tended to be 'harder' in this country than in the United States, as exemplified by Booth's resolution 'to make no use of the fact to which I cannot give a quantitive value. . . . My object has been to show the numerical relation which poverty, misery and depravity bear to regular earnings and comparative comfort, and to describe the general conditions under which each class lives'.[10] Thus the major British surveys until after World War II concerned poverty, family expenditure, housing conditions, diet, and, since 1936, radio listening. The major exception to this trend perhaps confirms the rule: in 1937 an organisation known as Mass Observation was founded with the aim of studying public opinion. Its impact was considerable at the outset precisely because it used less systematic quantitive methods in favour of impressions, quotations and overheard comments.

While the British survey movement focused on the incontrovertible statistics of the public's behaviour, two developments in the United States were changing the face of modern survey research. In the early 1930s, George Gallup and Elmo Roper separately set up research organisations to study public opinion using national sample surveys, thus taking up the challenge to quantify the 'softer' data of mass attitudes and opinions. Second, Paul Lazarsfeld and his colleagues demonstrated and conceptualised the distinctive methods of multi-variate analysis, the origins of which are to be found in Durkheim's 1896 study of European suicide rates, and Yule's 1899 criticisms of some of Booth's conclusions.[11] As Glock observes, 'Lazarsfeld's seminal contribution was to perceive and to make explicit the potential for using survey research in the social scientist's search for explanations.'[12]

Although, as we shall see, we can never strictly speaking determine cause and effect relationships between factors, there is a logic to survey analysis which enables us to say that a given factor can or cannot be eliminated as a possible cause of some effect. In the next chapters, we will examine some of the principles and procedures for classifying social data, interpreting its meaning, and unravelling causal relationships in the tangled complexities which constitute society and social relations.

Classifying, measuring and coding   2

When the fieldwork is completed and the analyst is faced with mountains of tatty questionnaires, he faces his most daunting moment. The task now is to portray the essential features in this mass of details. To do so the evidence has to be organised, categorised and processed. Competence at this stage is just as crucial as the earlier stages of deciding who was to be asked what in what manner. Mistaken decisions now may be almost as difficult to rectify later as a failure to ask the right people the most relevant questions.

The task will be less daunting if the purposes of the survey and the construction of the questionnaire have been carefully thought out. To the extent that the questionnaire has been pre-coded, the organising of the data for processing will be that much easier. In a pre-coded questionnaire, all the possible answers to a question are listed, so that the interviewer (or the respondent, when a self-administered questionnaire has been used) has only to check off the appropriate categories. But if there are open-ended questions (those not supplied with a selection of pre-coded answers), a systematic way of classifying the responses must be created and adhered to rigidly. The set of rules for classifying questionnaire responses is called the *coding-frame,* and the act of classifying is known as *coding.*

Only someone thoroughly conversant with the aims of the survey can construct the coding-frame, for the rules for classifying answers are determined by the purpose of the question. The answers to the apparently straightforward question 'What is your job?' would be very differently handled in coding if the intent was to identify the respondent's social class than it would if we were trying to assess how the demands of the job affect family life. In the former case, classification might be into categories derived from such criteria as manual/non-manual, earnings, degree of training required or social prestige; in the latter, hours worked, shiftwork, absence overnight might be taken into account.

Equally, as we shall see, coding requires well constructed questions. No amount of juggling with the coding rules can produce a satisfactory classification of answers to a badly worded question. In 1880 a questionnaire to over 25,000 French employers included the question, 'Give details of the division of labour in your firm'. There is no record that the results were ever analysed, perhaps because the investigator was defeated by the coding problems raised. His name was Karl Marx.[1]

PREPARING THE DATA

Preparing the data for processing becomes less daunting if a routine sequence of operations is undertaken. First, questionnaires must be numbered and checked. Then a coding frame must be drawn up to handle the responses to open-ended questions. Third comes the coding (which should include checks on the coding), resulting in a data matrix.[2] Fourth, tables giving frequency counts of all the coding categories for each question must be produced. This stage will probably involve transferring the data matrix on to cards of some sort or another for quicker tabulation. Finally, inspection of the frequencies may lead to decisions to combine different sets of categories together to form, in effect, new sets, or to combine some categories within sets to obtain more meaningful frequencies.

1. CHECKING

Every questionnaire must be numbered so that, if necessary, reference can be made to it later. It is common practice to incorporate into the identification number digits which incorporate some information about the respondent; for example, in a sample of university students the first two digits might indicate the faculty of a respondent. Alternatively, postal questionnaires are often numbered in sequence as they are returned. By comparing the answers of early and late returns the analyst may be able to infer something about the effect of 'volunteer bias' on the overall results. If a questionnaire was circulated to a sample of students and completed anonymously, a positive correlation between early returning and radical attitudes might be taken to suggest that non-respondents tended to be less radical, and that the sample finally obtained was biased in that respect.

Next, each questionnaire should be checked for completeness and accuracy. Every question should have been answered, even if the answer is 'not applicable'. Questions left blank might turn out to be unasked, unanswerable or inapplicable. When the check is done within hours of the interview, questioning the interviewer or a quick postal inquiry may resolve the issue. Inaccuracy in a questionnaire can often be spotted by inconsistencies between answers to different factual questions. A thirty-year-old with an old age pension cannot happen: other answers may give the clue whether age or source of income is correct. If the problem cannot be resolved satisfactorily, the answers to *both* questions should be changed to 'Not known'. A lot of inconsistencies may justify discarding the case from the achieved sample. Inconsistencies between opinion questions should of course not be altered since they may well reflect the respondent's opinions accurately. Unlike coding, checking must be done one questionnaire at a time, so that the checker has as complete a picture of the respondent as possible.

A record should be kept of the number of times each question raises problems for the checker. An excessive number may indicate that a question was misunderstood either by the interviewer or the respondent. If interviewing is still in progress, the matter can be clarified for interviewers, although this may create difficulties in comparing answers. If it is completed, responses to the problematic question should be treated with caution.

2. CONSTRUCTING A CODING FRAME

The results which make up a coding frame spell out the investigator's own frame of reference or context for understanding the data. He is directing attention to selected features of the data, deciding which aspects of the total body of information are to enter into his analysis.

These features may be qualities or quantities: attributes such as sex or marital status, or measured factors like age or earnings. Generically, they are variously called variables, factors, dimensions, attributes, by different writers. We shall adopt the general term 'variable' in preference to the others, each of which have more specialised meanings which will be defined at the appropriate point.

Classification and Measurement

To construct a coding-frame effectively, it is necessary to understand the basic principles of classification and measurement. All social research is based on the study of variables. Research ultimately must be based on comparisons, whether it be comparisons between different groups of cases, between the same case at different points in time, or even between what is and what might have been. While ethnomethodologists may try to study the constant, invariant features of social relationships, the only way they can do so is by comparing what happens when what is taken for granted is changed or made problematic. We can only understand what is universal by actually or imaginatively visualising its absence.

To compare, one must assess. Measurement, putting a numerical value to an evaluation, is but one type of assessment. The varied ways in which social researchers may find assessments formulated are exemplified in school reports.

Geography: Has worked better this term. Exams. 60%.

English: Satisfactory. Position in class: 14th out of 30.

Art: He has a genuine gift for art, and has produced some bold, imaginative work.

Music: He has no ear for music of any sort.

Woodwork: A true craftsman.

Number of times absent: 0. Number of times late: 3.

Each statement assigns a specific value for an individual on a given variable. Some of these values are quantitative—Geography exam 60%, English 14th out of 30, no absences, lateness: 3—while others are qualitative. For the latter, the specific qualities on each variable are attributes. His English has the attribute of being 'satisfactory', in art he is 'gifted', and his work is 'bold', 'imaginative'; in woodwork, he is 'a true craftsman'.

Were we now to have available all the reports for the same term of this student's classmates, we could categorise the variety of classificatory terms used. For the quantitative variables such as geography, we would learn what the actual spread of marks was within the limits of 0 to 100 per cent and thus more meaningfully compare 60 per cent with other geography marks.

Examining the variety of comments among the qualitative variables, we might discover that two kinds of assessments were used. Suppose that the English teacher has only used the terms, 'good', 'satisfactory', and 'poor', while in geography the comments included 'good', 'can do better than this', 'written work satisfactory, but maps ruined by untidiness', and 'should get at least C in "O" levels'. The English assessments can be graded on a scale with 'good' and 'poor' at opposite ends. All the pupils could be allocated to one of the three positions on this scale, and thus can be compared on the same criterion. They have been assessed in order of merit, just as has been done in a more precise way, with thirty scale positions, in giving each pupil's position in class. This variable, which at first sight seems to consist of a set of attributes, turns out to have some characteristics in common with a quantitative variable.

This is not so for the comments on Geography. They cannot be scaled or put into an order of magnitude. We cannot say who was better this term in Geography by comparing those of whom it was said 'Can do better than this' with those who 'should get at least C in "O" level'. If every pupil had been classified as 'satisfactory' in English, there would be no basis for comparison and hence, literally, no variable.

These examples outline the major types of variables into which all social data must be classified. Variables may be either quantitative or qualitative. Quantitative variables may be further divided into *ordinal* scales, *interval* scales and *ratio* scales. Qualitative variables—those which simply consist of a set of labels or names—are known as *nominal* scales. When a nominal scale has only two attributes (yes/no, over 21/under 21, right/wrong) it is described as *dichotomous* or binary.

To see why it is vital to recognise these levels of measurement, we

17

must understand the logical properties connecting data measured by each level. Taking the sequence nominal/ordinal/interval/ratio, the level of sophistication of measurement increases at each stage. Ordinal scales have all the properties of nominal scales plus certain others, interval scales all those of nominal and ordinal scales, and so on. The logical connections are thus cumulative in character. Although social scientists always prefer the highest level of measurement available for a variable, in practice the higher one goes the fewer indisputable examples can be found in social life.

Nominal measures. The most important level to the sociologist is thus the nominal level. Nominal data consists of the frequencies of sets of attributes. The nominal level of measurement is the act of categorising. The only logical relationship between the categories of a nominal variable is that of equivalence or similarity, or their opposites, non-equivalence or dissimilarity. Examples are sex, marital status, religion, leisure pursuits, types of mental illness. The categories of each of the variables are lists and we cannot say of any item on the list that it has more or less of some quality than any other, nor that one item is closer in similarity to another item than it is to a third. If, however, *all* the items in the list can be ordered, a higher level of measurement is being used. In nominal measurement, we can only say whether one instance is equivalent or not to another instance.

The marital status of one person can only be the same or different from that of another; one person cannot be more married or more single than another. If, on reflection, A does seem to be more single than B in the sense of being, say, a more confirmed bachelor, then the variable of marital status has subtly changed its meaning and is now being conceived of as an ordinal variable. This can easily occur, leading to inappropriate methods of handling the data.

The only statistic which can be used to summarise the average or central tendency of a nominal distribution is the most typical category, the one which appeared most frequently—the mode. The modal spectator sport in this country, for example, is football.

Another way of looking at nominal data, and one which can have certain advantages in statistics and analysis, is to break down a set of categories comprising a nominal variable into as many dichotomous variables as there were originally categories. Thus instead of the variable marital status being composed of the alternatives 'married', 'single', 'divorced', 'widowed', or 'not known', we have five variables, each with only two possible answers, yes or no. The advantages will be seen when looking at the descriptive statistics appropriate to each level of measurement; the main disadvantage is that we may lose sight of the fact that logically only one of the five variables can be true. Indeed, a computer analysis of the data, automatically tabulating everything against everything (a common form of mindless 'data-dredging') may excite and mock the analyst with empirical demonstrations that 'no A's are B'. To distinguish this kind of dichotomised variable and those in which the original question does permit more than one answer ('Name those of the following countries you have visited') we will call the former a member of an *alternative attribute set*,[3] and the latter *multiple mention sets*.

Alternative attributes are sometimes known in the trade as 'dummy variables', the products of 'one-zero measurement'. By allotting the quantitative values 0 (= absence of the attribute) and 1 (= its presence), many attempts have been made to obtain some of the sophisticated statistical advantages of metric measurement, most notably regression analysis (see chapter 5). While alternative attribute sets are assumed to be statistically independent, the elements of a multiple mention set are not independent. This must be remembered when statistical tests based upon assumptions of randomness are proposed.

Ordinal measures. In an ordinal measure, there is a logical order to the scale categories. Cases are compared and if they are not equivalent, they are ranked according to whether they have more or less of a quality.

To bring out clearly the properties of an ordinal scale, consider how you might assess the relative hardness of a number of substances. This can be done by seeing which substance can scratch which: by this test, putty is clearly softer than wood and wood than stone. Notice that it is unnecessary to test all combinations of substances; once we have established that stone scratches wood and wood scratches putty, it is a property of an ordinal scale (known as *transitivity*) that we can deduce logically that stone will scratch putty and not vice versa. Equivalence relations still hold since we may find two substances each of which is

19

equally hard (i.e. can scratch each other). Among the set of data, the appropriate measure of average hardness is the middle substance. In the rank order, putty—wood—stone, wood is the median.

This type of scale is very common in social life. We have, for example, pecking orders and hierarchies, power and prestige relations, the skilled, semiskilled and unskilled classification of manual jobs. Partly because the idea is so basic in common parlance, sociologists have devised a number of techniques for measuring social data at this level. It has been argued that this is the most appropriate level for social measurement, because the properties of an ordinal scale correspond to the properties of the phenomenon in the 'real' world of social reality. These techniques result in scales based on ideas analogous to that of 'social distance'.

When graduates are assessed in terms of first, upper second, lower second, or third class honours degrees, we know who obtained the better degree, but we do not know from this classification how much difference there is between the classes. The usual frequency distribution of classes would suggest that there is a bigger gap between a first and upper second than between an upper and lower second because it is probably harder to move from an upper second to a first than it is to move from a lower second to an upper second; hence equal intervals between classes cannot be assumed.

Metric scales: interval and ratio. In a metric scale not only is there equivalence among, and rank-ordering between, categories, but the interval or distance between each class is the same. The extra logical operations which can be carried out are those more commonly thought of as mathematical: addition and subtraction for interval scales, and addition, subtraction, multiplication and division for ratio scales. This is because a standard unit of measurement has been introduced into the process. The operations of categorising and comparing in nominal and ordinal measurements are based on the other cases in the same data set: a big fish may head the pecking order in a little bowl (if we may mix the metaphors), but we cannot say whether it is more or less dominant when compared with a similar sized fish in a big bowl. To do so requires a standard unit measure of dominance comparable to the pound or dollar in income, or the metre in length. It is possible to add the values in a metric distribution to obtain the mean as a measure of central tendency.

Income and intelligence quotients are social examples of interval scales. Strictly speaking, income is only an interval scale in societies with a monetary system in which slavery does not exist. This is because the distinction between interval and ratio scales is based upon the absence or presence of a non-arbitrary zero point. It is meaningless to speak of an IQ of zero: the absence of an IQ is conceptually a nonsense. Similarly, income can only take the value 'zero' in a country with slaves or peasants who maintain themselves solely from the produce of the land or sea. Measuring temperature on Fahrenheit or Centigrade scales are interval measurements, because the 0° readings do not mean an absence of any heat, but are simply arbitrary points. $0^{\circ}F$ was set at the coldest temperature which could then be obtained in the laboratory, the freezing point of brine, and $0^{\circ}C$ represents the freezing point of water.

The value 'zero' on a ratio scale means what it says, the absence of whatever is being measured. In the measurement of temperature on the kelvin scale, 0° means the absolute zero temperature, which would be equivalent to $-273^{\circ}C$. Because the process of multiplication and division can be legitimately used it is a more sophisticated kind of measurement than an interval scale. The ratio of two values expresses this; it is meaningful to say that doctors in the age group 35—44 are four times more at risk of death if they smoke at least twenty-five cigarettes a day than non-smoking doctors of the same age[4] since their respective mortality risks are 1.1 and 4.4 per thousand. Social data are often presented in this form, since basically it simply presupposes head-counting, which cannot result in negative frequencies. Age or years of schooling, literacy or crime rates, remarriages, or number of days lost through strikes are examples. As they indicate, ratio variables in social science are more likely to occur in demographic or administrative statistics than in attempts to measure sociological constructs like alienation.

Although interval and ratio scales are logically different, the uses which are made of them in social research rarely justify maintaining the distinction. Here we have lumped them together under the generic term, metric scales.

We can summarise the properties of each level of measurement, bringing out their cumulative logical character diagramatically.[5]

Property	Logical Relations	Level of measurement			
		Nominal	Ordinal	Metric Interval	Ratio
Classification	$= \neq$	+	+	+	+
Rank ordering	$= \neq < >$	−	+	+	+
Equal distance	$= \neq < >$ + − −	−	−	+	+
Zero = absence	$= \neq < >$ + − x ÷	−	−	−	+

Which statistics are appropriate?

It is not the aim of this book to repeat what can be commonly found in any statistic textbook. Surveys, however, cannot be analysed without statistics. Students often find a variety of methods available for calculating the same class of statistic and are at a loss to know which to prefer. With knowledge of the levels of measurement of the variables, the most appropriate statistic can be gleaned from Table 1.[6] In consulting it, two points should be borne in mind. When a variable can be interpreted at different levels of measurement, prefer the higher level because a lower measurement than is necessary loses some of the information which might otherwise be available. To treat as nominal what is properly ordinal is to reduce a set of transitive categories to a set of equivalence categories. Similarly, to treat as ordinal what is properly metric is to lose the possibility of quantifying how much difference exists between non-equivalent classes.

Secondly, and as a corollary, unless there are good reasons to the contrary, use the measure which does not appear in earlier columns. In other words, the mean is to be preferred to the mode or median for metric data, although to use either of the others would not be wrong. As an example of an exception to this rule, take the problem of the most appropriate measure of central tendency for an income distribution within a nation. The median income is usually given since most

TABLE 1
Statistics appropriate to nominal, ordinal, and metric data

Type of statistic	Level of second variable	Level of measurement		
		Nominal	Ordinal	Metric
Average or central tendency	–	Mode	Median mode	Mean median mode
Dispersion or scatter	–	% in the mode, % distribution (if not more than, say, 12 categories)	Interquartile range or percentile differences, Range	Standard deviation Variance IQR or percentile differences Range
Association and correlation	Nominal	Chi-square derivatives (χ) Phi-square (ϕ^2) (if both variables are dichotomies) Yule's Q Goodman-Kruskal's (τ_b) Lambda (λ)	Gamma (if the nominal variable is dichotomised)	Point biserial, if nominal variable is dichotomy
	Ordinal	Gamma (γ), if nominal variable is dichotomised	Kendall's tau (τ) Goodman-Kruskal's gamma (γ) Spearman's rho (ρ)	
	Metric	Point biserial (if nominal variable is dichotomous)		Product moment correlation

23

nations have a very inegalitarian distribution. The mean, unlike the median, is affected by all the values of the distribution, and hence may be pulled misleadingly upwards by a few relatively rare but enormously wealthy men.

When deciding upon a measure of association, the measurement levels of both variables have to be considered. As a simple guide, when both differ in levels, the higher level variable is considered as comparable to the simpler one. Never increase the level of the lower arbitrarily, since this will have the effect of giving the data spurious properties which it does not possess. It will be noted (if not already, certainly when you consult a statistical text) that the problem of the degree of association in tables involving nominal data has no simple solution. This is because, from the statistical perspective, each nominal variable is really a set of alternative attributes, or different variables. Hence there are many different associations in a multinominal contingency table, and to ask for a single statistic is to ask for a figure summarising all the different associations.

Principles of classification

A variable, it has been said, has four working parts: a name, a definition, a set of categories, and a procedure for allocating cases to categories.[7] The set of categories may be at any of the levels of measurement we have covered, and there are no intrinsic problems in allocating cases to categories when the categories are a set of quantitative values: i.e. where it has an ordinal position or a numerical value. With qualitative variables three general criteria must be followed in developing a good, nominal level classification system, whether the data be responses to open-ended survey questions, the contents of communications, or systematic observations of behaviour.[8] The purpose of the classifying operation is 'to distinguish elements which behave differently in terms of the problem under study'.[9]

Principle 1: Logical correctness. The set of categories developed must be exhaustive: every possible response must be classifiable into one, and only one, of the categories. This may mean that a 'waste-paper basket' category is needed, 'other answers', but the proportion of cases so classified should be kept to an absolute minimum since they represent an admission of defeat in classifying. This residual category should not contain more than 5 per cent (as a rough guide) of the answers, nor be larger than any other main heading.

The categories should also be mutually exclusive: only one category should be possible for any given response. What this means can best be shown by an example of a violation of the rule. In Lombroso's archaic classification of criminals as 'insane, born criminals, habitual, occasional, and criminal by passion', biological, genetic, temperamental and criminal career factors are combined into one set of categories. Many dimensions are lumped together into a single variable. As a set of rules it would be impossible to apply: a particular case might be correctly classified into four of the five categories at once, since only 'habitual/occasional' are mutually exclusive. In this example, Lombroso has failed to stick to just one classifying principle, or dimension, of criminality. Distinct variables have been mixed.

Principle 2: Articulated and alternative variables. In developing a classification system, the analyst often finds himself following two inconsistent paths; on the one hand, towards the smallest number of categories possible in the interests of clarity and economy and, on the other hand, towards retaining important distinctions in the data and not lumping together elements which are dissimilar. There are two ways out of this dilemma.

1. The first is to create a classification with a stepwise structure, starting with a few broad categories and progressively breaking them down into finer, more detailed categories.

In this way, one can eat one's cake and have it too: when a few broad categories are sufficient, only the simple first step need be used; when a more detailed step is required the finer distinctions can be found preserved in the later, finer steps of the classification system.[10]

As an example of an *articulated* classification, in a survey of secondary school pupils in Uganda, the writer asked, 'What kind of job do you expect to do after leaving school?'[11] In classifying the answers, a two-step system was decided on in order to preserve in accessible form the two substantive elements: type of work, and the level of education or training implied by the students' answers. The manifest content of the answer, type of work, forms the first, cruder, step of the system, and the implied content the second step. Answers which cannot be classified at this level can still be usefully accommodated into the manifest level classification.

2. It may be more convenient to set up *alternative variables* depending upon an earlier answer. Often the questionnaire will have been designed to facilitate this. At the analytic stage, how the data was obtained is not at issue; the problem is how to present it. As an example of an alternative variable approach, consider a question asked in a national survey of primary school children's parents.[12] The questionnaire reads:

... which of these do you think is better?

RUNNING PROMPT
For the quicker and slower children to be mixed together in one class   1 ask (*a*)
or
For the quicker to be put in one class and the slower in another   3 ask (*b*)
Don't know, no opinion, can't generalise, depends entirely on child   2

(*a*) *If better for quicker and slower to be mixed (1):*
What do you think are the advantages of having the quicker and slower children mixed together in one class?

CODE ALL THAT APPLY
Avoids feeling of difference and of brighter/quicker looking down on slower/duller   1
Gives a sense of competition, spurs on the slower/backward   2
Others (specify)

(*b*) *If better for quicker and slower to be separated (3)*
What do you think are the advantages of having the quicker in one and the slower in another?

CODE ALL THAT APPLY

The slow ones can have more attention/tuition; can be brought
on   1
The bright child is not held back academically by slow children,
teachers can give time to bright child   2
Slow children are not made to feel slow/dunces/ashamed   3
Helps the teacher, makes life easier for the teacher   4
Others (specify)

The results are actually presented in three tables corresponding to the
main question, 'Whether parents prefer streaming by ability' and two
alternative variables, (*a*) 'Advantages of streaming by ability' and (*b*)
'Advantages of mixed ability classes'. No parent could appear in both
alternative variables, and of course the total number of parents
answering each must equal the relevant subtotal of the main variable.

TABLE 2

*Whether parents prefer streaming by ability or not by father's
occupation*

Q.28 Parents' preferences	Father's occupation			
	Non-manual		Manual	
	%	(N)	%	(N)
For quicker and slower children to be in one class	28	(245)	28	(608)
For streaming by ability	67	(586)	65	(1414)
No preference, depended on child	5	(47)	7	(152)
TOTAL	100	(878)	100	(2174)

Source. Tables 2 and 3 are adapted from The Plowden Report, vol. 2,
tables 60–62, p. 142.

Note that more than one category may be needed to code an answer,
and thus the frequency totals may be more than the numbers of

respondents. This violates the rule of mutual exclusivity, in the interest of retaining the texture of individual responses more accurately. Generally, multiple mention sets should be avoided if possible, because they introduce confusion into the interpretation of findings by giving equal weight to each part of an answer when respondents may not do so in their own minds. Also, the frequency distribution of multiple mention answers may reflect the opinions of the more loquacious and articulate respondents. For example, non-manual parents gave more reasons supporting their preference than did manual worker parents, regardless of what that preference was (Table 3 (*a*) and (*b*)). These problems might be avoided by asking respondents to rank order their preferences. If this has not been done, the analyst should at least give an indication of the frequency distribution of 'number of answers given'.

In Table 3 are shown (*a*) the 'articulated classification' and (*b*) the 'alternative variables' solutions to the economy/relevance problem. Parts (*a*) and (*b*) may look very different from each other, but inspection will show their close similarity: (*a*) expresses the data in (*b*) in a slightly reduced form, with the figures emphasising the distribution of reasons for one preference or the other in the total sample.

TABLE 3

(*a*) *Whether parents prefer streaming by ability or not, and their reasons for their preference, analysed by father's occupation*

	Father's occupation	
	Non-manual	Manual
Parents' preference, and reason	%	%
For quicker and slower children to be in one class, because	28	28
avoids feeling of difference	10	10
gives a sense of competition,	18	19
brighter children can help the slower to develop	4	5
other reasons	6	3

Table 3 Continued

	Father's occupation			
	Non-manual %		Manual %	
For streaming by ability, because	67			65
slow ones can have more attention	42		46	
bright children not held back	40		35	
slow children not made to feel ashamed	21		19	
makes life easier for the teacher	10		8	
other reasons	2		2	
No preference, depended on child	5	5	7	7
TOTAL		100		100
(N)	(878)		(2174)	
Total number of reasons (%)	158		154	

(b)(i) *Advantages of quicker and slower children in one class, by father's occupation*

	Father's occupation	
	Non-manual	Manual
Reason for preferring 'mixed ability' classes	%	%
Avoids feeling of difference	39	36
Gives a sense of competition	66	68
Brighter children can help the slower to develop	13	18
Too early to judge child's abilities at this stage	7	2
It steadies the quicker ones	5	2
Streaming is unfair to slower children	8	5
Other reasons	2	2
Total	140	133
(N = 100)	(244)	(608)

(ii) *Advantages of streaming by ability, by father's occupation*

	Father's occupation	
	Non-manual %	Manual %
Slower ones can have more attention	62	71
Bright children not held back	65	54
Slow children not made to feel ashamed	31	29
Makes life easier for the teacher	15	12
Other reasons	3	4
Total	177	170
(N = 100)	(588)	(1420)

To cut down the number of categories in the table, reasons given by 3 per cent or less of the sample have been merged into residual 'Other reasons' categories. Table 3 (*b*) requires two sub tables to show a fuller version of the same data, with the figures emphasising the distribution of reasons for preferences within each preference grouping, instead of among the total sample.

Principle 3: The relationship with theory and data. Many variables are made up of categories which form part of the language of everyday discourse. Most face-sheet variables by which the sociologist categorises respondents are simply taken over from those things we generally need to know to place another person in everyday life: sex, age, marital status, nationality, region of origin, social status. With the exception of the last, the sociologist uses the common parlance categories of everyday life. Similarly, he is not going to waste time thinking up new principles for classifying, say, the various mass media, or modes of transport, without special reasons.

When the variables of interest do not have self-evident values, sets of categories must be developed, from theory, from intuition, or from the data itself. A survey which sets out to test a theory, such as the attempt to test Michel's law of oligarchy in *Union Democracy*[13], must use categories related to those in which the theory is framed. The theoretical concepts should determine the data which is collected and the manner in which it is classified. The relationship between theory and data is one of *coding-down*, from the theory to the respondents, by imposing a framework over their replies.

When the purpose of the analysis is descriptive rather than hypothesis-testing, our concern will be to discover the main varieties of opinion and behaviour in the sample. In this case, the data determines the classifications which emerge. Here, the relationship between description and explanation, on the one hand, and data on the other, is one of *coding-up*. This is much more problematical, and the remaining discussion of coding is largely concerned with coding-up.

An equally important consideration is *comparability* with other studies. If a study is to contribute to developing an understanding of social life beyond the particular circumstances it has investigated, findings must be clearly comparable with other investigations. It would be meaningless, for example, to compare the relationship between social class and, say, leisure activities in samples of two different populations, if one author had used the Registrar-General's Classification of occupations and the other had used subjective, self-assigned class. Later investigators need not defer to earlier measures as though they were sacrosanct, they need only obtain data which allows both comparable measures and their own preferred measure to be used and compared. To encourage comparability, the British Sociological Association publish a series which discuss alternative ways of assessing and classifying such variables as household composition, education and income.[14]

The source of classifying principles

It might be assumed that in the continual debate between the positivist and the *verstehen* approaches to social research, the social surveyor would back the positivist all the way. He is, after all, committed to the view that objective knowledge can be achieved regardless of the subject matter, and that the interaction between the observed and the observer can be minimised so that their mutual influence on the data is negligible. By contrast, the *verstehen* proponent denies the possibility of such minimising and argues that it is the inquirer's duty to 'get inside' his subjects, to explain attitudes and behaviour in terms of their own explanations and understandings.[15]

Levels of explanation. But there are two ways in which the classical mainstream in social surveys corresponds more closely to the *verstehen* approach, both generally unrecognised. First, objectivity is not something immutable in time and space, now and for ever more. It is a standard to be aimed at, but only partially achieved, in the processes of classifying according to some useful criterion. As Lazarsfeld and Barton say:

> It is certainly possible to make human judgement *somewhat* [their italics] objective by systematising the training and instructions of classifiers as much as possible. . . A classic example . . . is the procedure used in judging horses. . . .

> The 'general appearance' of the draft horse is now given a weight of 29 points, and this is subdivided into 'weight', 5 points, 'form', 4 points, 'quality', 6 points, 'action', 10 points and 'temperament', 3 points. The scorer goes over the horse, noticing in detail all the points specified, and he marks down opposite each his judgement of the degree to which the horse before him is deficient in that particular point.

> The reader who is unfamiliar with draft-horse judging will be aware that these are hardly instructions which anyone could follow and come to the same judgements; the rules work only when there is a common body of understanding as to what is meant by the various terms and what represents good and bad characteristics.[16]

As changes gradually occur in what is expected of a good horse, so will the judgments of experts, and until a new set of criteria are agreed, the objectivity, as measured by agreement between judges, will decline.

Analysing reasons. Second, the same authors insist on the need to categorise data in terms of 'the structure of the situation' and 'the respondent's frame of reference', which we may loosely equate with coding-down and coding-up respectively. While it is useful to distinguish analytically between the two, the distinction may be difficult to make in practice.

'Adapting to the structure of the situation' means trying to bring out the essential elements or dimensions in the phenomenon under investigation, this essence being determined by the framework and purpose of the inquiry. One of the most difficult kinds of question to classify is that which asks why people behave in the way they do, because for every behaviour there are so many levels at which one can produce reasons. In a market research study of women's reasons for buying cosmetics, open-ended answers might be classified by a scheme which included as dimensions, sources of information on the product, how the customer wishes to appear ('impression management', in Goffman's term), whom she wishes to impress, cost, problems of applying the cosmetic, etc. Each may be an element inherent in the buying decision which can be intuited from introspection and general knowledge in drawing up, as well as in analysing, an interviewing schedule.

> The reason the comments would fit is that the scheme of classification matches the actual process involved in buying and using cosmetics. These are the processes from which the respondent herself has derived her comments; the classification, so to speak, put the comments back where they came from.[17]

Social scientists often accept as a sufficient explanation of why people behave as they do, the 'hard' facts of their life histories. Voting, for example, is 'explained' by showing that Labour votes tend to be working-class, male rather than female, less educated and less upwardly mobile. In doing so the reasons given by the respondents themselves are accorded less weight than these more deterministic factors. This preference may follow from the analyst's theoretical stance, his theory of action, but it may also have been reinforced by traditional methods of analysing social surveys. Thus an informant's opinion may not be accepted at its face value, but taken as a surface level indicator of a deeper, unifying attitudinal dimension. Scaling procedures for constructing measures of latent dimensions treat the manifest responses as their raw materials, with the result that deviant opinions or individuals are reduced to 'error'. This means that the opportunity to study deviant responses will have been lost. Similarly, the accounts an informant offers for his own behaviour are interpreted as a consequence of his age, sex, social class or IQ and hence are regarded as of little theoretical interest as an explanatory variable. They are rarely seen as intrinsically interesting as variables mediating between the informant's sociological position and his individual behaviour. Instead, they are relegated to the role of one of an indefinite number of variables which are not equal when the rule is enunciated that, say, 'other things being equal, men who left school by fifteen and have always had manual jobs tend to vote Labour'.

One reason for this failure is that the act of classifying reasons leads at once to the problem of deciding what a 'real' reason is. As Kadushin points out,[18] there are in fact no 'real' reasons, unless one can specify the level of explanation required. A 'real' reason is simply one that is theoretically relevant. In attempting to explain why an individual sought psychotherapeutic help, a biochemist might be satisfied to find an endocrinal deficiency, a psychoanalyst that the individual had unresolved hostilities to his parents, a behavioural psychologist that he had inadequate social skills, and a sociologist that he was subject to incompatible role expectations. Kadushin shows how an accounting scheme for reason analysis, in this case why people have emotional problems, can be developed with close similarities to Parson's paradigms of action. He develops a multidimensional scheme, focusing on the individual's situation, his perception of the attributes of his situation, the way he evaluates them, his values, and his social interaction with others. Systematic application of this accounting system results in four typologies of how people came to recognise their problems: (*a*) those who had them pointed out by others, (*b*) those who recognised the psychosomatic nature of their illness, (*c*) those with marital conflict, and (*d*) those who recognised for themselves their state resulted from an accumulation of mishaps.

If we examine the rules set up by the author for classifying 'types of decision', it becomes evident that they embody a theoretical order of precedence.

Both social pressures operating on the individual and his own perception of the attributes of the problem were considered. If social pressures were such as to inform the individual that he had a problem before he himself realised it, a type (*a*) called 'told by others' was first separated out. Of the remaining persons, attributes of the problem were then considered. If the problem was described as one which involved physical symptoms, a second type, (*b*) 'physical symptoms', was screened out. The persons remaining after this screening were examined and the attribute of perceiving one's problems as marital was considered. All the remaining persons who described their problem as one of 'marital conflict' were thus distinguished as a third type (*c*). Finally (*d*) 'self-realisation' remains as a residual category which nevertheless correctly describes the persons who remained after the first three types were withdrawn.[19]

The principle underlying this priority theory is based on the direction of pressures to the self, that social pressure is most likely and introspection least likely to be effective in inducing recognition of one's problem. Because the classification reflects the principle, rather than a set of isolated categories, the rules for classifying are spelt out in the report. Without the rules the categories would not of themselves have been mutually exclusive; one can easily imagine cases in which more than one category applied.

Kadushin then goes on to show how this classification makes sense of the data, how each group is related to different ways of conceptualising their problems, which in turn influence the chances of a client being accepted for, and remaining in, treatment. Those who were 'told', and those who diagnosed themselves, located the problem in themselves, while almost none of the 'marital conflict' group blamed themselves. This 'physical symptom' group also located the problem in themselves, but in their bodies rather than their minds. The 'marital conflict' group were least likely to be accepted for treatment, and most likely to drop out if accepted, as might be expected of those who denied their own responsibility for their problems. Equally, the group most inclined to consider their problems as one of their own making, the 'self-diagnosed', were most readily accepted and least likely to drop out. Thus the original classification is shown to have theoretical validity, since the data corresponds to the predictions which could be deduced from the theory. To this extent, the 'real' reasons have been identified.

Zeisel has outlined some standard structural schemes for 'reason analysis'—the process of classifying explanations given by respondents for their actions.[20] Reason analysis should not be confused with causal analysis: in the former, reasons are sought from individual respondents;

in causal analysis, 'causes' are more akin to forces acting on groups of individuals in certain circumstances. The following paradigms illustrate some ways of structuring answers to the question, "Why?" As an 'open' question, it should be used sparingly in interviews because it usually produces incomplete and ambiguous answers from the analyst's viewpoint. With forethought, guided perhaps by these models, the most appropriate scheme for one's research objectives can be foreseen, and questions can then be framed to cover the relevant elements.

Reason analysis schemes

Types of models and their applicability in classifying reasons

Model	Elements	Typical situations for use
1. Push-pull	Attributes of X, attributes of Y	Migration from X to Y, Changing a preference from item X to item Y
2. Attributes —motives —influences	Attributes of X, motives of respondent, channels of influences over choice	Open-ended list of reasons for choosing X
3. Technical properties — resulting gratification.	X's technical properties, satisfying effects for respondent	'What is it about X that you like?' (e.g. 'I go to Spain for my holidays because you can be sure of the sun [technical property] and I want to get a good tan' [satisfaction].)
4. Obstacles — culprits — fatalism	Barriers to change, who's to blame, resignation to one's lot	Explaining lack of needed changes
5. Underlying reasons — precipitating cause.	This adds a time factor to any element in 2 or 6	'Why did you act *just* then?' (e.g. 'We always wanted a bigger car and then we got a bit from Premium Bonds.')
6. Motive — means — opportunity	Actor's motives — resources available — occasion arose	Explaining an unusual action, 'Why *ever* did you do that?' (also the detective's checklist in all whodunits)

These schema and the kinds of situations in which they seem appropriate are, of course, only suggestive. There is no necessary connection between the two; they are simply strategies which have repeatedly been found useful in analysing respondents' reasons.

It is in requiring category systems to be adapted to the respondent's frame of reference that Lazarsfeld and Barton link themselves most nearly to the *verstehen* approach. Yet they do so, not from any prior commitments to the issues of the debate, but from the practical demands of the data itself. Their stance has been influential in the survey field because, handled imaginatively, and with deference to respondents' views, the survey is well suited to the job of feeding back to society not simply how many people align themselves with this or that opinion, but also what other viewpoints exist. The pity is that in the rush to interview, careful pilot studies are so often omitted, and in the rush to count results, precoded closed questions which may distort the respondents' intended opinions are used. Quantification should not mean that the respondent's own definition of the situation, the way in which he perceives and interprets the topic of questioning, is ignored.

Just what this means in practice can be seen by comparing the streaming question, and especially the limited number of precoded answers, with the relative wealth of different answers actually obtained, in Table 3 (*b*). Evidence of careful pilot work to identify the main dimensions of parents' frames of reference is shown by the fact that the precodes correctly account for the most frequent responses. At the pilot stage, 'advice was sought from heads and other teachers in primary schools, care committee workers, and child welfare officers. Discussions were held with four groups of parents and freely-ranging individual interviews with approximately fifty parents.'[21]

As well as pilot studies, in which a sample of the prospective survey population are questioned in the role of informants rather than respondents, the Gallup 'Quintamensional plan of question design' is often recommended as a way of avoiding feeding respondents with preconceived answers to attitude questions.[22] This covers five aspects of opinion conditions: the respondent's awareness of the issue, his general attitude, his attitude to specific aspects of particular interest to the researcher, his reasons for his answers, and the intensity with which

37

he holds the opinion he has given. In practice, most of its benefits are lost if respondents are not categorised in a manner which takes account of the pattern of their five responses as a whole.

Developing classifications from the data

The process of developing a classification system (or coding frame) after questionnaires have been completed is straightforward. A sample of the materials to be coded is selected, using any method of selection which seems likely to maximise the variety of responses it contains. The aim is to ensure that the selection comprises a set of examples of each type of respondent, not necessarily a representative sample of all respondents. Twenty are probably enough to start with.

The open-ended responses are then typed out on separate sheets, so that they can be physically sorted into appropriate groups. This should result in fewer groups than cases sampled, but the reduction may be slight. Then continue taking small samples, typing out, allocating to category groups, revising and resorting as necessary until a stable set of categories has emerged, with only very occasional unclassifiable answers being found. When categories seem to have become stable, the principle underlying the allocation to categories must be spelled out explicitly and unequivocally so that others (who may be coders or the eventual reader) can, in practice or imagination, classify cases with results equivalent to those of the coding-frame constructor. These 'spelled-out' principles become the coding instructions.

It often helps to clarify the coding instructions by asking a series of questions of the data to which only yes or no answers can be given. Depending on the answers, either the response can be allotted to a code category at once, or a further question can be put to it in the same way. This method, analogous to the creation of a flow diagram, traces a path through the data until a single code category is reached, and hence cannot be used when multiple coding is permitted. In practice, it may also be more appropriate when the analysis requires the coder to draw inferences from the manifest response, rather than classifying it at its face value. Kadushin's classification of the reasons patients gave for their decision to seek psychotherapy follows this sequential process. It will almost certainly help in defining each category to give examples of the kinds of answers it incorporates, as has been done in Table 3 (*b*).

This stage of analysis is the most crucial, in the sense that it will cause the most difficulty to correct errors or change decisions about the coding-frame. If categories have to be revised after the actual coding has started, it cannot of course be done in mid-stream; it will be necessary to recode those already completed with the new scheme.

With the advent of 'package' programs for analysing surveys on computers, coding frames can be drawn up which postpone the need to make final classifying decisions until all the answers have been inspected. Briefly, the strategy is to forget the usual need to reduce the number of categories to a maximum of about twelve, and to code the answers into as many categories as seem necessary to do justice to the range of responses given. The first run of the data through the computer should be used to obtain a frequency distribution of the many-category variables. Knowing the empirical distribution of answers may then suggest ways in which the many categories can be combined into a comprehensible smaller number. Most survey packages have facilities for recoding the data into new variables, without having to repunch the data. Chapter 3 has a further discussion of the technical aspects of these operations.

3. THE CODING PROCEDURE

The process of coding may appear to be a routine mechanical task, easily delegated to assistants. This should not blind us to the dangers of doing so, which immediately become apparent in the following coder's story.

There didn't appear to be much concern with the possibility of inconsistency among the coders. Various coders used various methods to determine the code of an open-ended question. Towards the end of the coding process, expediency became the keynote, leading to gross inconsistency. The most expedient method of coding a few of the trickier questions was to put down a '4' (this was the middle-of-the-road response on the one question that had the most variation). If the responses were not clear or comprehensible,

39

the coder had two alternatives: on the one hand he could puzzle over it and ask for other opinions or, on the other hand, he could assign it an arbitrary number, or forget the response entirely.

In the beginning, many of us, when in doubt about a response, would ask the supervisor or his assistant. After a while, I noticed that quite often the supervisor's opinion would differ when asked twice about the same response and he would often give two different answers in response to the same question. One way the supervisor and his assistant would determine the correct coding for an answer would be to look at the respondent's previous answers and deduce what they should have answered—thereby coding on *what they thought the respondent should have answered* [original italics], not on the basis of what he *did* answer. . .

Some coders expected a fixed pattern of response. I, not being sure of what some responses meant in a total political profile, treated each response separately—which I feel is the correct way of coding a questionnaire. Others, as I learnt through their incessant jabbering, took what they thought was a more sophisticated method of treating an interview. A few would discuss the respondent's answers as if they took one political or social standpoint as an indicator of what all the responses should be. They would laugh over an inconsistency in the respondent's replies, feeling that one answer did not fit the previous pattern of responses.[23]

Roth's article goes on to suggest that informal restrictive practices and deviations from the rulebook are as normal a practice in social research as they are in other areas of mass production. Due to its mechanical nature, the hired hand 'is simply expected to carry out assigned tasks and turn in results which will "pass inspection"', the inspection itself often being carried out by another hired hand.

Major social surveys, of their nature, cannot be undertaken without delegating much of the work involved. This does not mean that Roth's comments can be discounted (although he suggests this would be the proper reception for studies in which hired hands played a significant part). Probably any sensitive researcher with experience of interviewers and coders will recognise the seriousness of the problems he raises, even if they can rarely be quantified.

In one small scale study of eight coders working on the same questionnaires (without, of course, knowledge of how the others had coded the items), total agreement was achieved between all eight in 88 per cent of the comparisons of questions in which there was no scope for coders' individual judgment. When comparisons were made of the coding of questions of open-ended questions, agreement between coders was only obtained in an average 43 per cent of instances. Furthermore, when asked to recode fifty schedules again, one-fifth of the open-ended questions were coded differently on the second occasion by the same coders.[24]

The *actual* practice of coding as opposed to the coding instructions, is the Achilles heel of the survey process. Few checks can be carried out by those responsible for the survey before substantive conclusions are drawn on the findings, and even fewer are available to the persistently sceptical or discerning reader. Internal contradictions in the data, such as married infants, are likely to be picked up and corrected in the data analysis stage. In any case, such errors are clearly careless in origin, and thus by definition are likely to be randomly distributed in the data if not discovered. Errors resulting from a fairly consistent policy by coders to treat ambiguous answers in a particular way, whether it be by assigning a neutral code or deducing 'what they should have answered', will result in a consistent bias in the data. This bias, it is reasonable to suppose, will be in the direction of conformity to expectations towards 'normality' in the cases of 'ordinary' citizens and towards coders' stereotypes in cases of which the coders have little personal experience themselves. Survey research has not been well served by those practitioners who have assumed that errors of all kinds will, in the long run, cancel themselves out. (An example can be found even in Lazarsfeld's writings. Discussing the relative influences on consumer behaviour, he writes: 'The analyst may assume that, if he over-rates the role of advertising in some cases, he will under-rate it in others so that the statistical result remains valid.'[25]) The nature of coding biases may be part of the reason why social surveys so rarely produce unexpected findings.

Certain measures and checks can be taken during coding to improve the process. Assistants should be carefully trained and rehearsed in the use of the coding frame, and, if possible, involved in the process of constructing it. A log should be kept of all queries to identify the more problematic questions, showing the question number, the response, the coding decision made, and the coder. The identity of the coder should also be coded as a variable of the questionnaire so that the coding can be done again if a particular coder's work turns out to be unreliable. Coding should not be done directly onto the questionnaire, as this would prevent any re-coding being done 'blind'.

Coding should also be done variable by variable, and not case by case. This serves two functions: it prevents the build-up of an image of the respondent which can determine the coding of ambiguous answers, and it enables the coder to comprehend more quickly the rules for coding each variable.

Ideally, each questionnaire should be coded by two different coders, working without knowledge of the other's decisions. These are then compared and discrepancies should be settled by the survey director if possible, by reference to the questionnaire. When a computer is to be used, there may be programs available which not only identify discrepancies, but show the alternative decisions in each case, the frequencies with which each coder is involved in a discrepancy, and the frequencies of each variable resulting in discrepancies. Deviant coders, it should be noted, are *not* necessarily the more errant ones; they may simply be more conscientious, independent, or isolated from the private coding norms developed by and shared between other coders.

Reliability and validity

By developing an explicit set of rules which minimise the use of personal judgment in classifying data, we hope to obtain coded data in which the classifying is unaffected by who did it or under what conditions. In the last few paragraphs we have seen that this is, in practice, very difficult to achieve. To the extent that this failure occurs, we speak of a classification being unreliable. Reliability is not of course an either/or phenomenon; if we could measure reliability we would not dismiss evidence which was marginally unreliable—we would simply take into account, in drawing conclusions, the degree of unreliability.

In practice we often can estimate how reliable our coded data is. The assessment of reliability has been gone into in great detail in the social sciences, especially in the field of psychometrics, the measurement of mental and personality characteristics. There, reliability is generally broken down into four types, depending upon the kind of factors disturbing a 'pure' measurement:

1. Observers may disagree when assessing the same phenomenon.
2. Assessments made by the same person or test of the same phenomenon on different occasions may differ.
3. Samples of the same phenomenon may not result in the same assessment.
4. Different indicators (or symptoms) of the same phenomenon may not result in the same conclusion.

Conceptually, then, the sources of measurement error (unreliability) are variations between observers, over time, between samples, and between items taken to indicate a characteristic. While the different sources may be theoretically distinct, in practice they are likely to occur together, and in social science the assumption that the phenomenon being assessed remains constant is especially risky. Estimation of the relevant kinds of reliability should also be attempted in social research and some ingenious techniques have been developed for doing so. Since the concepts of reliability and validity are a meeting-point of statistics and methods texts, we need not go into technicalities here.[26] Some general points must be mentioned.

The key to the analysis of social surveys, as of other forms of evidence, is the constant attempt to eliminate explanations which are plausible alternatives to that favoured by the investigator. The analyst must learn to play devil's advocate with his most cherished theories: the more convincingly he can show alternative explanations to his own to be implausible, the more impressive become his own theories. Questions of reliability and validity are among the first possibilities to be raised. Is this result due to weak or unreliable measurement? If not, is it perhaps due to the measure assessing something other than what it is supposed to measure? In other words, is the measure or classification valid?

A measure is valid to the extent that it in fact measures what it is supposed to be dealing with, and not something else. How can we measure such elusive concepts as happiness, social status, gregariousness or self-esteem? Perhaps by asking people about themselves in ways which permit us to characterise each of them relative to others on our concept. But in questioning, ostensibly in ways which provide data for inferences about their standing on the concept, we risk tapping something more like defensiveness or 'presentation of self', to use Goffman's phrase. Hence the need for empirical checks on validity.

Although the two are not totally independent of each other, validity and reliability are conceptually quite distinct. Let us take a clock as an example. A clock is valid in so far as it tells the correct time. If it is consistently five minutes fast it is to that extent invalid, but it remains reliable in the sense that different observers will agree on what time it tells (inter-observer reliability). If, however, it starts to gain, and hence becomes increasingly invalid, its instability is a new source of unreliability since the difference between the true time and the time it gives varies on different occasions. A luminous clock which has lost most of its luminous paint may well result in loss of inter-observer reliability in the dark, since different observers may not agree on what it says.

Nearly all techniques for estimating reliability and validity result in correlational measures. Sociological scales and psychometric tests are quoted as having, say, an inter-observer reliability of 0.85, where 1.0 would indicate perfect reliability and 0.0 the complete lack of any consistency between observers. It must be remembered, however, that such coefficients vary, and are only indices of how reliable a measure was in the particular circumstances of that measurement. Each study should therefore demonstrate its own reliability and validity measures or arguments.

Validity arguments can take a number of forms, none of them in the nature of things conclusive. A measure is valid to the extent that it measures what it is intended to measure. If the construct were directly measurable, like absenteeism, the question of validity would not arise. The problem has to be faced in the more usual situation where an indicator is taken as an indirect measure of a construct. Absenteeism, for example, might be intended to act as an indicator of morale in an industry, which cannot itself be directly measured. Thus validity measures can never in practice be perfect even if reliability is perfect, because a validity coefficient of 1.0 would mean that we were measuring the indicator itself, not the underlying construct it stands for.

In general, four distinct types of validity are usually distinguished, but none can ultimately bridge the gap between an indicator and its indicandum, the theoretical construct. These four are derived from two questions: does it make sense? and does it work?

If the indicator-data we obtain is related to another variable in the way which we would expect its underlying construct to be, then it begins to make sense to regard indicator and construct as meaningfully equivalent.

As a practical example of how an author satisfies himself and hopefully, his reader, of the reliability and validity of a measure, let us look at the measurement of self-esteem in Rosenberg's *Society and the Adolescent Self-Image*. For practical reasons, a self-administered questionnaire which students could complete quickly and anonymously was necessary. The author defines self-esteem to mean, for his purposes, 'the feeling that one is good enough. The individual . . . respects himself for what he is but he does not stand in awe of himself nor does he expect others to stand in awe of him'.[27] A selection of attitude statements which dealt openly with self-esteem in both a positive or negative way were chosen, using as a criterion the maximising of a reliability measure which ensures that the statements belong to the same dimension. 'There is little doubt that the items deal with a favourable or unfavourable attitude to oneself', but the author is not satisfied to rely solely on this appeal to face validity. Since there are no criterion groups available known to be characterised by a given level of self-esteem, relationships are examined between whatever is being measured and other measures expected, on theoretical grounds, to be positively associated with self-esteem. As expected, a low self-esteem score is associated with appearing to be depressed, feeling discouraged, exhibiting psychosomatic symptoms of anxiety, being inconspicuous among peers, and feeling that others have little respect for oneself.

45

CHESTER COLLEGE LIBRARY

While no one of these findings could be regarded as clinching the validity argument, the presence of them all makes validity plausible and puts the onus of disproof on those who would challenge this interpretation.

Indicators and indices

Only rarely can we find a simple item which can reliably be used as the sole indicator of a concept. Putting all one's eggs in one basket is always risky, particularly in social research, where a single item can be so unreliable. Important concepts are usually assessed by indices, in which several items are combined. This will almost certainly increase both the reliability and validity of the parent concept measure.

The construction of scales and indices is a complex matter which may not justify the effort in social research. We have seen that most of the work on reliability and validity has been carried out in psychometrics, where some action often follows from the use of a test. The consequences of a wrong decision are much more serious than is the case in most social research, where

the consequences of using a single item instead of a scale may simply be to attenuate the correlation between two variables say, from 0.30 to 0.30. Who can measure the social costs of such an error? Furthermore, if the social researchers were to use a small number of long scales, like the psychometrician, he would have to forego a large number of single items that he might otherwise study, and this might well be more costly than the reduction in reliability.[28]

We take up the discussion of indices more fully in Chapter 4.

With the data coded and checked according to the coding frame, the analyst will want to see what his material holds in store for him. At this stage no new information on his sample can be obtained; analysis can only classify what is already there. If he is dissatisfied, another inquiry is the only way to remedy his unease.

The basic vessel for storing sorted and ordered data is of course the table. Good habits in producing and handling the tables will ease the analyst's task at each stage. To develop these habits, it helps to understand the anatomy of a table.

TABLE CONSTRUCTION

Every table consists of five parts: title, stub, caption, body and supplementary notes. Tables lacking part of this anatomy are not hard to find in survey reports, but they are not recommended as models. Table 4 illustrates these parts.

Title normally includes a table number and a title showing the contents of the table *completely* and *clearly*. The contents are usually arranged in the order, 'What, how, where and when'. If more information is needed, a bracketed note under the title is sometimes used.
Stub and caption. The stubs and captions each contain as a heading the name of the variable, and may also have subsequent subheadings, followed by the categories of the variable. A 'Total' column appears as the first or the final subheading in the stub or caption. If the categories are groupings of a quantitative variable it must be clear where the dividing lines occur. Thus if the variable were 'age at starting school', the categories might be 'under 4', '4 but under 5', and '5 and over'.

TABLE 4

Road death rates in six European countries 1969   Title

<table>
<tr><td>Country</td><td>Vehicles per 100,000 population</td><td>Road deaths per 100,000 population</td><td>Road deaths per 10,000 vehicles</td><td>Caption</td></tr>
<tr><td>Gt. Britain</td><td>26</td><td>14</td><td>5</td><td rowspan="6">Body</td></tr>
<tr><td>France*</td><td>40</td><td>32</td><td>8†</td></tr>
<tr><td>Netherlands</td><td>35</td><td>24</td><td>7</td></tr>
<tr><td>Belgium*</td><td>27</td><td>30</td><td>11</td></tr>
<tr><td>Germany</td><td>24</td><td>27</td><td>11</td></tr>
<tr><td>Italy*</td><td>24</td><td>19</td><td>8</td></tr>
</table>

Stub (applies to Country column) / Body (applies to data rows)

Source. Adapted from *Road Accidents, 1970,* H.M.S.O., 1972, table 30.

Notes. * Most countries define a fatality as being due to a road accident if the death occurs within thirty days of the accident. Some countries, however, limit the fatalities to those occurring within shorter periods. The rates above are based upon figures adjusted as described below to represent standardised thirty-day death rates.

Country	Definition	Approximate correction made (%)
Belgium	At scene of accident	Increase by 100%
France	Within 6 days	Increase by 9%
Italy	Within 7 days	Increase by 7%

Supplementary notes

† 1968 figure

The body contains the figures summarising the data. These are usually frequencies or percentages, but may also be statistics like rates, averages or correlation coefficients.

Supplementary notes. Every table should include a note on the source of the data. If the table is simply for the analyst to work from, but not for publication, the source would serve as a check on the columns, and perhaps groupings of the rows, of the data matrix. In the example the source note shows where the figures for numbers of vehicles, road deaths, and population have been obtained.

Other matters of fact may need to be drawn to the reader's attention, such as adjustments to the data or varying definitions, which need to be considered when comparing figures.

Tables are generally of two kinds, *analytic* or *repository*. Table 4 is analytic because it has been constructed in order to draw the reader's attention to a particular feature; such tables are usually supplemented by a linking commentary in the text discussing this feature. Tables which simply house the raw material for subsequent analyses and interpretations are inventory or repository tables. The statistical reports of government departments, or of the Census, are largely composed of repository tables giving the results of straightforward counting operations. Such tables are not normally given in social surveys, because the reader expects an analysis and interpretation of the data to be presented for him. However, it is a cardinal rule of all survey tables and reports that the original numbers should be deducible from the evidence published.

More usually, survey report tables will present percentages rather than raw numbers. Percentage tables must always show the base number which constitutes 100 per cent; the reader then has the safeguard that he can reconstitute the original figures for his own purposes. If the figures do not total 100 per cent, an explanation should be given: this is likely to be either that some respondents gave more than one response or, if the total is very close to 100 per cent, due to rounding.

Opinions differ on the rounding off of decimal points in percentages. Some analysts favour showing one decimal place because the final digit can be adjusted to ensure that all percentages total 100.0 per cent, even though in reality rounding causes them to sum a fraction above or below 100.0 per cent. To report these odd totals would serve only to confuse many readers. Others, including the author, prefer to report percentages rounded to the nearest whole number and to show the total as 100 per cent even if the rounded values actually total 99 per cent or 101 per cent. When this occurs an explanatory note should be added, as in Table 4. Rounding to whole numbers makes the table much easier to read, and does not give the impression of more precision than the numbers warrant. (When a percentage ends in exactly 0.5, statisticians prefer to round the percentage to the nearest even number, instead of always rounding up or down. In the long run this will eliminate any bias in one or other direction.) Only in samples of several thousand would differences of less than 1 per cent be statistically significant. A sample survey never justifies reporting percentages to two decimal places.

In general, tables should be as self-contained as possible: they should be self-explanatory, without it being necessary to refer to the surrounding text. Many readers prefer to obtain the gist of a survey's findings by reading the tables only, drawing their own interpretation from them. C. P. Scott's dictum that 'facts are sacred, comment is free' is nowhere truer than in a survey report, with the additional proviso that *all* the facts of the variables displayed must be shown in the tables.

Finally, table readers need, and will appreciate, the maximum consideration from the authors. Analytic tables should need a minimum of effort from the reader to see those features the analyst wishes to highlight. A table should not attempt to highlight too many features; it is preferable to construct extra tables to show additional features.

TABLES OF ONE, TWO OR THREE DIMENSIONS

One-dimensional tables, the straight counts of a variable, are only the first stage of analysis. Their utility is limited to giving an idea of the basic raw material available. The analyst should scan the 'straight counts' with an eye to the kind of analyses which they permit. Are there enough cases of certain types of people to permit meaningful comparisons between them? In the Plowden Report's national survey of parents of primary school children, the authors noted that nearly half the families with income less than £10 per week (in 1964) were one-parent families, but because there were so few motherless families they were unable to compare motherless with fatherless families on their child's school record.[1]

If there are not enough cases, there may be ways of combining categories without their becoming so gross or heterogeneous that they lose their usefulness. For example, the Plowden researchers asked parents what kind of secondary school they hoped their children would go to. Because a small proportion of the answers covered a fairly wide range of grammar school alternatives, they found it convenient to dichotomise the data by, in effect, rephrasing the question to, 'Do parents want grammar schooling for their child or not?' In combining categories to form new subgroups for comparative analyses, the ideal for statistical efficiency is equal sized groups but not, of course, at the expense of meaningfulness. If 50 per cent of a sample were middle-aged, 40 per cent young and 10 per cent elderly, the split should be made between 40 per cent young, 60 per cent others and not 50 per cent middle-aged, 50 per cent young or elderly.

Every questionnaire contains the responses, 'no answer', 'don't know', 'others', 'unclassifiable', 'not applicable' and the like. Should they be inserted as category responses or not? The answer lies in whether the response is regarded as a substantive one or not. A person who says he doesn't know, or gives an answer which does not fall neatly into one of the main categories is nonetheless answering the question, and such cases should be included in the frequency distribution. Respondents to whom questions are not applicable should be excluded from tabulations of those variables and the size of the sub-sample so created should be clearly shown.

Where the information is not known or unclassifiable, decisions on handling missing data also depend upon the purpose of analysis. If the main objective is to describe the parent population, the full sample must be retained. By juxtaposing the variable containing the missing information with a series of other variables, some idea of what is missing can often be obtained. For example, in the Plowden survey, social class emerges as a significant factor in explaining a variety of influences on children's reactions to school. In classifying parent's social class, a small proportion are unclassifiable when the father's job is taken as the criterion. The analyst must query whether the missing information is likely to distort his findings. The Plowden researchers found fewer 'unclassifiables' (1 per cent) in their sample of fathers than were reported in the last Census figures for married men aged 20–64 (3 per cent) in the population. Further analysis of these few showed that the 'unclassifiables' included an exceptionally high proportion of working mothers, and fatherless children. Thus, a substantial meaning can be inferred about the 'unclassifiable social class' group: many are from families without a father living at home.[2]

Alternatively, if the objective is to analyse the relationship between specified variables, cases should be excluded whenever information is missing on the variables being compared. Any generalisations about relationships need then to be made in two stages. First we must ask whether the excluded cases distort the sample, and then whether we can generalise the results from the reduced sample to the original, or a reformulated, population.

Two-dimensional tables are probably the most frequently found in surveys, because they show the relationship between two variables without confusing the clarity of the picture by bringing in other dimensions, however relevant. Frequencies, percentages, rates, or descriptive statistics form the body of the table, showing how a set of cases are grouped by two or more criteria simultaneously instead of only one.

Typically, the two-dimensional table (otherwise known as a 'cross-break' or 'cross-tab') shows the joint frequency of the distribution of two nominal or ordinal variables in a form which facilitates the analysis of relationships. In Table 5, for example, the relationship between where a man was born and where he works is shown for a sample of 350 residents in a hypothetical community. The frequencies for each variable are given in the *marginals*. In reading such a table, one starts from the marginals and works inwards to the bivariate body of the table. Here, the marginals tell us that a larger majority of the sample work locally than were born in the district.

TABLE 5

Residents' place of work, by place of birth

Place of work	Locally born	Born elsewhere	Total
Locally	100	140	240
Elsewhere	100	10	110
Total	200	150	350

Source. Hypothetical.

If there were no connection between where a man works and where he was born we would expect to find equivalent proportions of each column in each row cell. As the table stands, this comparison has to be carried out by the reader. Roughly two-thirds (240/350) of the men in this community work within it. The proportions are very different in the two columns for the birthplace categories. Half the locally born work here, but the vast majority of the non-native residents work in the locality. Hence the two dichotomous variables, locally born and working locally, are correlated.

Percentaging two-dimensional tables

Leaving the reader to make these calculations by mental arithmetic is hardly being considerate to him. He would probably prefer the figures presented as percentages rather than frequencies. But in which direction should one percentage; by rows, by columns, or taking the total sample of 350 as the base?

Generally, we can eliminate the final method. Percentaging on the grand total is, in effect, to recast bivariate data into univariate form, or an *index*. Table 5 would become a single variable taking four values, as in Table 6.

TABLE 6

Bivariate data recast as an index (%)

Native-born, local worker	29
Non-native, local worker	40
Native-born, non-local worker	29
Non-native, non-local worker	3
TOTAL (N = 350)	100*

*Total sums to 101 per cent due to rounding.

More usually, the decision as to which variable to percentage is determined by the point the analyst wishes to emphasise. Tables are constructed to show how one variable (the *independent* or 'causal' variable) affects the other (the *dependent* or 'effect' variable). The general principle is to use the total number of cases in each 'causal' category as the base (= 100 per cent), showing the 'effects' as percentages. It helps both in percentaging and writing the commentary to tables to remember that the base categories will usually be the subject, and the categories of the dependent variable, the verbs or object in describing findings.

In the present example, the dependent variable is place of work since in some sense it depends on place of birth. Place of work cannot in any sense cause or determine one's birthplace. Percentaging accordingly produces Table 7.

TABLE 7

Place of work, by birthplace

Place of work	Place of birth	
	Local	Elsewhere
	%	%
Locally	50	93
Elsewhere	50	7
TOTAL	100	100
(N)	(200)	(150)

In an easier form, this table brings out the conclusion we drew from the raw figures. Half the locally born also work locally, compared with 93 per cent of those not born in the district. It is unnecessary to give the marginals of the dependent variable, place of work, since this additional information would tell the reader nothing essential to his understanding of the analytic point being made.

TABLE 8

Birthplace, by place of work

Workplace	Place of birth			
	Local	Elsewhere	Total	(N)
Locally	42	58	100	(240)
Elsewhere	91	9	100	(110)

To complete the picture Table 8 contains the same data, this time percentaged across. The first row shows where residents who work locally were born. In the second row, showing that residents working outside the district were predominantly locally born, it is not clear what sociological meaning is given which would not be better indicated by percentaging in the column direction. 'Nearly all newcomers work in the district' makes more sense than 'Commuters are nearly all born in the district'.

Frequently, either variable can be regarded as dependent on the other, according to the questions being asked of the data. Take, for example, the two variables, attendance figures at a football team's matches, and its performance throughout the season. Attendance, arguably, is determined by the quality of the game people expect from the team's recent performances. Or the team's performance may be boosted by the support they are given. The analyst would need to examine percentage figures calculated in both directions to determine whether one, both, or neither hypothesis were true.

It is conventional to phrase the title according to the formula, 'Dependent variable by independent variable(s)'. The category totals of the 'by' variable(s) thus provide the base figure on which to percentage. These numbers must always be presented; this is often done by showing them in brackets as above.

When the reader's attention is drawn to only one category of a variable, perhaps because it is a dichotomy like 'yes/no', tables can sometimes be abbreviated for simplicity. Table 7 could be shown, without losing any information, as:

% of locally born who also work locally   50 (N=200)
% of those born outside the district who work locally   93 (N=150)

Because the percentages given do not add up to 100 per cent, it is essential to show that they ought *not* to do so by supplying the base numbers in the groups being compared.

Multivariate tables

Most two-dimensional tables are likely to pose more questions than they solve. Why are these two variables related? or, alternatively, why aren't they? Is the link between them only true in certain circumstances, or for certain kinds of people? Can it be regarded as part of a cause and effect sequence, or is it perhaps a meaningless association due to their being different effects of a common cause? If they cannot be dismissed as meaningless, what are the adjacent links in the causal chain?

The strategies for resolving such questions will be discussed in the final chapter, but they are best understood through the three (or even more)-dimensional table. In the three-dimensional table, the relationship between two dimensions is tabulated for each category of a third variable. This gives as many two-dimensional subtables as there are categories in the third dimension.

Suppose that we feel that the relationship between work place and birthplace can be partly explained by where a respondent's wife was born. Classifying her birthplace like her husband's as local or elsewhere might give the results shown in Table 9.

TABLE 9

Husband's workplace by husband's and wife's birthplace

Wife born:	Locally		Elsewhere	
Husband born:	Locally	Elsewhere	Locally	Elsewhere
Husband's work-place	%	%	%	%
Local	58	88	38	98
Elsewhere	42	12	62	2
TOTAL	100	100	100	100
(N)	(120)	(68)	(80)	(82)

Introducing the third variable has added to our understanding of the data. Looking only at the top row (since the lower row can be inferred from it), we see that the 50 per cent of the locally born men who also work locally can now be split into 58 per cent if they married a local girl, and 38 per cent if they married an outsider. Similarly, in virtually all (98 per cent) of the couples born elsewhere the husband works locally, compared with 88 per cent of the couples in which only the wife is locally born. In fact, only two (2 per cent of 82 to nearest whole number) of the 350 men sampled do not have at least one of the three local links with the community which have been examined.

A three-dimensional table contains a great deal of information, most of it implicit. Besides the three relationships between the three pairs of variables known as the marginal relations, there are all the comparisons within the trivariate data. We turn to these in the final chapter. Before temporarily leaving the subject, note that the three-dimensional table can be generalised to the multidimensional table. But, just as it is difficult to locate things in the 'real' world in more than four dimensions (taking time to be the fourth) so it is rare to find more than four-dimensional tables in practice.

Although tables are the most effective way of communicating quantitative information to an innumerate readership, many defeat their own purpose by providing too much information. In a three-dimensional table with each variable dichotomised, there are eight cells to inspect. While not all analysts are as happy to reduce reality to a series of dichotomies as the influential group associated with Paul Lazarsfeld, we must recognise how quickly and easily multivariate tables become unmanageable. A three-dimensional table in which each variable has five categories would have 125 cells. A similar four dimensional cross-tabulation would produce 625 cells. Only a national Census would have enough cases to fill so many cells, and the reader would, not unreasonably, expect the Census interpreters to make the data more manageable. Ways of reducing the data are discussed in the next chapter.

THE HARDWARE OF SURVEY ANALYSIS

With a respectful nod to Durkheim's assistant who alone classified 26,000 suicides separately according to their age, sex, marital status and number of children,[3] we can safely assume that few analysts will eschew mechanical aids to producing tables and statistics. The choice is between three methods: hand tallying, punched cards on a simple sorting device, or computer analysis. Even assuming that one has access to a countersorter and a computer, the choice is not automatic.

The three considerations are the number of questionnaires completed, the number of variables to be extracted, and the complexity of the analysis proposed. Perhaps one person handling 200 or 300 simple questionnaires with the analysis limited to a series of two-dimensional tables is the limit to handwork. One would hope that two or three of the variables would be common to all the tables. This design is the most usual: looking at the relationship between a small number of independent variables like age, sex and socio-economic status on a variety of attitudes and reports of behaviour.

Hand tallying

At its simplest, hand tallying is done by physically sorting the questionnaires into piles of common responses or attributes, and counting them. Where a series of cross-tabulations are based on a common variable, the common variable should be sorted first and retained; the counts for different variables are then made per pile, using prepared skeletal tables.

A relatively quick method of tabulating with smaller surveys and few variables is to use ordinary index or post cards, one per respondent. Each variable is alloted an area of the card, in which a letter, number or other symbol represents the category of the response. With an effective layout using colours, circles, underlining and so on, with the most important independent variables in the more prominent positions like corners and edges, cases can be sorted or counted almost as quickly as playing cards.

The number and complexity of the sorts required will determine whether the time spent in transferring questionnaire contents to cards is justified. When the total number of *categories*, not variables, is small it may be convenient to use edge-punched cards. These are punched with holes around all four edges; each one representing an attribute. Again using one card for each case, the presence of each attribute is recorded by clipping into the hole from the edge. When all the cards are stacked together, those with an attribute can be sorted from those without it by sticking a knitting needle through the appropriate hole and lifting the entire deck. The clipped cards will fall' out, and can either be counted or even weighed to obtain frequencies.

Punched cards

In five circumstances it is probably worth while transferring coded data on to standard 80-column punched cards. In most surveys of a reputable size, at least one will apply:

— when the number of variables is large,
— when the number of questionnaires is more than 200 or 300,
— when the analysis requires statistical calculations other than percentages, or three/or more dimensional tables,
— when the data needs to be checked for internal consistency, and otherwise 'cleaned up' before analysis,
— when the data needs to be transformed after the marginal frequencies have been inspected, either by combining variables to form new ones, or by combining categories within variables.

In the last three situations, a 'package' program (sic) on a computer would be advisable to take over most of the donkey work.

Punched cards are devices by which computers can recognise digits, letters and punctuation marks. Most are printed with 80 columns, each consisting of the numbers 0 to 9, with two blank areas at the top of each column. When holes are punched in certain combinations, into the printed digits and the extra areas, the computer can read a column to mean a number or a character. Figure 1 shows a card punched with the characters which have been *interpreted* at the top of each column. The conventions by which holes are coded into characters is not quite universal among all computers; the letters A to Z and the digits 0 to 9 are standard, but the punctuation marks and symbols such as £ and % vary. Cards are usually punched and interpreted simultaneously on a keyboard machine looking like a large typewriter, although they can be handled much more slowly on a small portable punch which neither interprets nor feeds cards automatically.

The origin of punched cards illustrates their usefulness in social surveys. The 1880 United States Census took seven years to complete the counting by hand. The Census Bureau were required by the Constitution to conduct a census every ten years in order that electoral districts could be apportioned fairly. As the population was then growing by one third every decade, a situation arose in which the next Census results might not have been published before another was due.

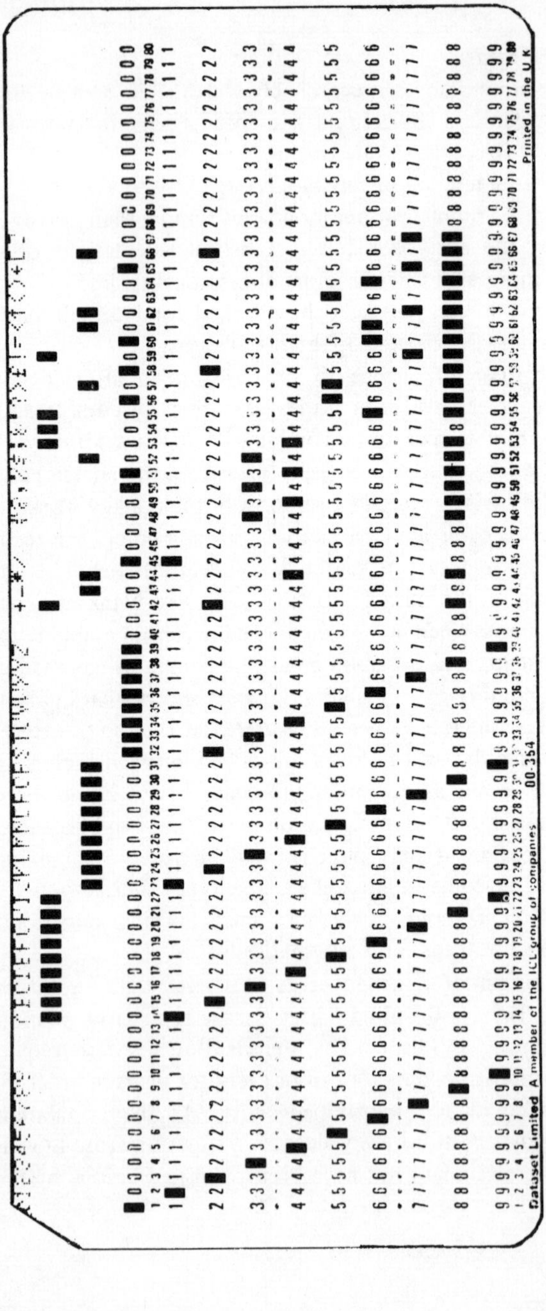

Fig. 1. An interpreted, 80 column, punched card.

60

A public competition to help the Bureau was won by Herman Hollerith. By adapting techniques used in the pianola and the Jacquard weaving loom, which are both regulated by paper holes representing tunes and patterns, Hollerith devised a tabulating machine which counted electrically holes made by an ordinary conductor's punch on special cards.[4] A contemporary described the scene in the counting room of the 1890 Census:

> As one enters, the ear catches the sound of crisp bell ringing, for all the world like that of sleighing. This music comes from the Hollerith machines on each of which ... a bell rings every time a card is counted, while its failure to ring indicates there is something wrong with the card or that it has not been slipped in properly.[5]

The codebook

In survey use today one or more cards are allotted to each case, and one or more columns to each variable. Assuming for a moment that all the data from a questionnaire can be fitted on to one card, then the same numbered columns on all cards are used to convey information on the same coded variable to the computer. Each variable is allotted its own column, or set of columns, in which the holes always represent the categories of that variable. It is conventional to use the first columns of each card to identify the case reference number. This set of columns, or *field*, has as many columns as there are digits in the highest reference number.

All the information linking variables to card fields, and holes within columns to categories of the variables, is stored in the *codebook*. It might begin:

Reference number	punch on cols 1–3
Sex	Column no: 4
Male	punch 1
Female	punch 2
Not stated	punch 0

Q.1   *Age* (to nearest year)   punch on cols 5 and 6:
       No information   punch 00

Q.2   *When did you last go away for at least two nights?*   Col. 7
       Within past month   punch 1
       One to six months   punch 2
       7 months to one year   punch 3
       13 to 24 months   punch 4
       2 to 5 years   punch 5
       Over 5 years   punch 6
       Never   punch 0
       No information,
         don't know   punch 9

Q.3   *How did you travel?*
       (No information, punch 9 on cols 8–14)
       walked only, no vehicle punch 0 on column 8:
       Used a vehicle: for each mode of travel punch 1 on:
       Bus, coach   column 9:
       Private car, taxi   column 10:
       Train   column 11:
       Plane   column 12:
       Boat   column 13:
       Other   column 14:

Notice that the answers to Question 2 are mutually exclusive and can therefore be allotted to a single column. Answers to Question 3 may include any number or combination of the different means of travel, each of which requires its own column. Ages (Question 1) will be given in two figures, so this variable needs a single card-field extending over two columns.

The codebook is the end-product of the coding-frame. Once an exhaustive list of all possible answers has been compiled, each variable is allotted a card field and the data from every questionnaire is transferred to punchcards for analysis mechanically on a countersorter, or electronically on a computer.

It is as well to know which type of machine is going to be used before allocating card fields and hole punches. Each has its advantages and disadvantages, which complement the other. The countersorter sorts and counts about 400 cards a minute on a given column. To produce a contingency table showing the breakdown of sex by Question 2, on the opposite page, the column indicator would be set to column 4, placed in a hopper, and 'run'. This would sort all the cards punched 1 on column 4 (to mean 'male') into the '1' pocket and the 4/2 cards into the '2' pocket. Then the indicator would be set to column 7, the 'sort' switch set to 'off' and the 'count' switch set to 'on'. Running each deck of cards separately would provide a count of the holes punched in column 7. Being unsorted this time, the cards would fall into the same pocket so that they could remain in their 'male' and 'female' decks ready for further tables relating sex to other variables.

The advantages of the countersorter are its simplicity, its speed relative to handwork and, to many researchers, the confidence they gain by being able to see the process by which cases become the frequencies in table-cells. With eighty columns and twelve possible holes in each, the card can hold 960 items of information per case. Complications arise, however, if more than one card is necessary for each case. This commonly happens with surveys collecting financial information, for example, because to record an income response would require a five-column field (three digits for pounds and two more for pence). To group income into a maximum of 12 categories may mean losing more information than is tolerable. Variables which spread over more than one column, like age in the example shown, should be avoided in countersorter work, since they create sorting problems. Surveys destined only for the countersorter often get round this by *multipunching* columns, squeezing more than one variable on to a column at a time. Question 3 might have been coded on to column 8, with a hole allocated for each method of transport used, instead of spreading expansively over seven columns. To have done so would, however, have put severe constraints on the analysis, since it would be impossible to count the different combinations of transport used; we could only say how many had used each one.

Computers cannot readily unscramble a multipunched column unless all the multipunchs happened to correspond to one of the fifty or so combinations of holes representing an *alphanumeric* character. Thus a computer analysis will normally mean more columns, and probably more cards per case, for each *record* than will a countersorter orientated codebook.

Survey analysis package programs

It is emphatically not necessary to learn how to program a computer in order to use one to analyse a survey. 'Package' programs have their instructions recorded in the computer; the user simply supplies four types of information:

1. Definitions of the data: the number of cases and cards per case, the number of variables and the card field they are punched in, the location of the case number, the names to be given to variables and their categories, which categories are to be excluded from analysis because they represent data missing for such reasons as refusals, don't know, not applicable.
2. Definitions of the tasks to be performed: which variables are to be cross-tabulated, percentaging instructions, what statistics are to be calculated, instructions on recoding, transforming variables, selecting subsamples, weighting data.
3. The survey data itself, correctly sequenced.
4. Job control information: each computer has its own system for getting jobs started, run, and finished, which only the local computer management can supply. The kind of information needed for job control will be the user's identity and authority, the name of the package program he is calling upon, and perhaps the maximum length of time to allow the program to run, and the peripheral devices needed to run the job.

There are, it has been estimated, perhaps six to nine hundred survey analysis packages, usually written to serve the needs of a particular computer or user. They are known by acronyms like OSIRIS, SALY, ANSWER, BMD, MVC, SDTAB, and ASCOP. A basic understanding of one makes others very much easier to master; here we describe the

SPSS (Statistical Package for the Social Sciences) which, together with BMD, leads the field. SPSS is available on twenty-one types of computer and is probably used several million times a year.[6]

Its capability can be discussed under two headings, data storage and retrieval, and analytical procedures. Survey analysis usually involves repeated looks at the same data in different ways. The sheer amount of information collected means that the data must be stored in a manner which makes it easy to get at, easy to handle, and difficult to alter by accident. SPSS allows the definition data and the survey data to be stored permanently by the computer, so that subsequent runs can be made knowing that the same data, defined in the same way, will be used. Variables can be recategorised or new variables treated by appropriate instructions, and analysis can be limited to subsets of the data: a random sample, or only cases with certain characteristics, for example. New information on old cases can be added to the data without resubmitting the new and old combined, which is particularly useful in longitudinal studies.

There are seven classes of analytical techniques available:

(a) descriptive statistics and histograms on any variable, together with frequency counts and percentages, fully annotated making it possible to have a complete description of the data akin to a codebook with frequencies included.

(b) contingency tables of up to ten variables simultaneously, again fully annotated and with a variety of statistical measures of relationship; or means and variances on one variable can be obtained for subgroups classified on up to five other variables. We could examine, for example, the average income and its distribution on subgroups simultaneously divided into age, sex, occupation, education, and size of household categories.

(c) without producing the associated tables, the program will calculate correlation matrices of sets of variables, using product-moment correlations for interval level data, or rank order coefficients for ordinal data. Missing data is handled either by excluding from the entire correlation matrix cases with any data missing, or by excluding cases only for the specific correlations in which data is missing on either variable.

65

(d) partial correlations, which are measures of association between two variables within subgroups of further variables.

(e) multiple regression analysis in which, analogously to a multi-dimensional table, the dependence of one variable upon a number of others is estimated, including measures of how much weight each carries, either alone or in combination with others.

(f) Guttman scalogram analysis for the construction of indices and scales which have the important social scientific properties of making use of nominal level data, and of being cumulative (as in social distance scales) and measurably unidimensional.

(g) factor analysis and principal component analysis.

In addition to these existing facilities, an enhanced version of SPSS is expected in 1975.

For full details the reader is referred to the authors' manual.[7] Here we will give an introductory outline on how the data and tasks to be performed are defined. The method is somewhat like completing a form with the difference that very few questions are compulsory; in the main, one answers only those questions that one chooses to ask.

Both the data and the task definitions are entered into the SPSS system on *control cards,* which have two parts: a *control field* covering columns 1 to 15, and a *specification field* covering the remainder of the card. The user punches into the control field key words which are analogous to a question on a form. He then punches his reply into the specification field.

Figure 2 shows a set of instructions which would (a) group the age data into five categories and a missing data group, (b) produce a codebook with frequencies for all variables, and (c) tabulate the age groups against a created variable summarising the travel patterns of each respondent and calculating chi-square for each table.

In the data definition section only four cards are mandatory; the rest are optional extras like excluding the 'Don't knows' and 'no information' cases from tables and calculations (MISSING VALUES control card), naming the variables (VAR LABELS) and the values in each variable (VALUE LABELS) so that they appear on the printed output, and regrouping the age variable into a limited number of meaningful

Figure 2: AN SPSS PROGRAM

	Control field	Specification field
	RUN NAME	EXAMPLE SURVEY ON TRAVEL PATTERNS
Mandatory	VARIABLE LIST	REFNUM, SEX, AGE, VAR001 to VAR008
	INPUT MEDIUM	CARD
	#OF CASES	65
	INPUT FORMAT	FIXED (F3.0, F1.0, F2.0, 8F1.0)
	RECODE	AGE (0 = 1) (1 THRU 16 = 2)
		(17 THRU 21 = 3) (22 THRU 30 = 4)
		(31 THRU 59 = 5) (60 THRU HIGHEST = 6)
	COMPUTE	TRAVPAT=VAR003*100000 + VAR004* 10000 +
		VAR005*1000 + VAR006* 100 +
		VAR007
	MISSING VALUES	SEX (0) / VAR003 TO VAR008 (0) /
	VAR LABELS	VAR001, WHEN LAST AWAY MORE THAN 2
		NIGHTS/VAR002, DID YOU USE A VEHICLE /
		VAR003, DID YOU USE A BUS OR COACH /
		VAR004, DID YOU USE A CAR OR TAXI /
		VAR005, DID YOU USE A TRAIN /
		VAR006, DID YOU USE A PLANE /
		VAR007, DID YOU USE A BOAT /
		VAR008, DID YOU USE ANY OTHER VEHICLE/
	VALUE LABELS	TRAVPAT (0) NO VEHICLES USED
		(100) PLANE ONLY
		(11000) CAR AND TRAIN
		(11100) CAR, TRAIN, PLANE
		(100001) BUS, OTHER
		(100100) BUS, PLANE/
		AGE (2) UNDER 17 (3) 17 − 21 (4) 22 − 30 (5)
		31 − 59 (6) 60 AND OVER (1) NOT KNOWN /
	PRINT FORMATS	REFNUM TO TRAVPAT (0)
	CODEBOOK	SEX TO TRAVPAT
	READ INPUT DATA	
	CROSSTABS	TRAVPAT BY AGE
	OPTIONS	3, 5
	STATISTICS	1
	FINISH	

categories (RECODE). The function of the VARIABLE LIST is to instruct the system on how many variables to expect and how to identify them. The identification is either by short, mnemonic labels of the user's choice or a numbered sequence supplied in the form VARx to VARy. The system also needs to know where to read the case data

67

from; besides cards, the data might be stored on magnetic or paper tape, disc or some other medium (INPUT MEDIUM). It needs to know when to stop interpreting incoming signals as survey data and to start expecting another control card; this need is met by telling it how many cases to expect (# OF CASES). Finally, the location of each variable on each case card has to be specified (INPUT FORMAT).

This specification may present some difficulty at first to users unfamiliar with the computer language FORTRAN. The word FIXED before the bracketed elements means that the variables are always to be found in the same position within each case. (The reader is not encouraged to try the alternative, FREEFIELD.) Within the brackets, the *format list* tells the system whether each variable is to be read as a number (as all are in the present example) or as *alphanumeric* characters. This nominal scale type of variable can take values which are either alphabetic letters or other characters; the latter may include numbers. Postal codes are an example: the numbers in the letter-number combinations are simply treated as if they were extra letters. It also informs the system of the card and column location of each variable.

The meaning of the format list in Figure 3 (F3.0, F1.0, F2.0, 8F1.0) is understood in conjunction with the *sequence* of variables in the VARIABLE LIST:

Figure 3   Format and variables

Variable name	Field width (cols)	No. of cols to right of decimal point	Therefore location is columns:	Item in the format list
REFNUM	3	0	1 to 3	F3.0
SEX	1	0	4	F1.0
AGE	2	0	5 and 6	F2.0
VAR001	1	0	7	
VAR002	1	0	8	
VAR003	1	0	9	
VAR004	1	0	10	8F1.0
VAR005	1	0	11	
VAR006	1	0	12	
VAR007	1	0	13	
VAR008	1	0	14	

The program automatically associates the first variable in the VARIABLE LIST with the first specification in the format list, and moves on over the number of columns indicated as the field width (the number immediately following the F). It allocates as many decimal places to the number it has read as the second figure in the specification instruction. The second variable in the VARIABLE LIST is then associated with the second format specification, and so on. When the program is run, a message is printed saying how many variables were expected (according to the VARIABLE LIST) and how many will be read (according to the INPUT FORMAT); if the two do not match, the user should recheck both specifications.

This ends the compulsory section of the data definitions. The task definitions begin with a RECODE data modification card, which groups the age data obtained in the survey into six categories so that it can be tabulated more readily. These new categories are then labelled and the 'no information' category which takes the value 0 is declared as a missing value.

Multiple answer questions

It was suggested earlier that one advantage of countersorter data-processing over computer analysis was the ability to code more than one answer on a card column, and hence to handle questions with more than one answer. The usual way to handle such questions on a computer is to regard each answer as an alternative attribute, describing the presence or absence of a property, or, in the statistician's language, as 'dummy' variables to be coded 0 to 1.

This is often unsatisfactory, because it inaccurately reduces the data to an alternative attribute set, implying that the pattern of responses given are unrelated and of no intrinsic interest. Take the six modes of travel listed in the coding-frame example. Multipunched or treated as dummy variables, both the countersorter and the computer would provide the frequencies with which each was used, but not the frequencies of *patterns* of use; we would not be able to find out how many people travelled by bus *and* train, for example. Although the SPSS system could be instructed to search for all possible combinations, this would take $2^6 = 64$ IF instructions. Besides being tedious, this would severely limit the number of other kinds of data modifications which could be carried out.

An alternative way in which patterns of responses can be produced uses the COMPUTE facility of SPSS by which new variables can be calculated from the basic variables. A new variable, TRAVPAT, is created from the six variables (VAR003 to VAR008) which indicate the use of particular types of vehicles. Each variable is multiplied by a different factor of 10, and the total aggregated. This gives a unique value to every observed pattern which can be counted and cross-tabulated like any other variable.

CODEBOOK is the instruction which generates frequency distributions, percentages, histograms and descriptive statistics for any variables named in the specification section of the control card. At this point, the program is about to carry out the instruction, without waiting to find out what other tasks it may be asked to do later. READ INPUT DATA tells the system that the next cards contain the survey data, which are then read and stored within the computer for the remainder of the current run. (It could also be instructed to FILE the data for a subsequent run.)

After successfully reading the sixty-five cases it finds a new instruction to produce a table, showing how the variable created by the program, TRAVPAT, is distributed by AGE. The tables are slightly modified by the user to give percentages down the columns (OPTIONS 3 and 5 delete row and total percentages) and STATISTICS 1 produces chi-squared and the number of degrees of freedom in the contingency table. Figure 4 shows the result of the CROSSTABS instruction.

The final instruction FINISH is self-evident.

This short account of SPSS cannot do justice to the flexibility of the package, nor mention all its capabilities. The manual[7] is painstakingly clear and written with the newcomer in mind. The package is already implemented at most British university computer centres. The program in Fig. 2 was completed in nine seconds on Nottingham University's 1906A.

Figure 4 EXAMPLE SURVEY ON TRAVEL PATTERNS

CROSSTABULATION OF TRAVPAT TYPES OF VEHICLES USED   BY AGE

COUNT COL PCT	AGE UNDER 17	17—21	22—30	31—59	60 AND OVER	ROW TOTAL
TRAVPAT	2.	3.	4.	5.	6.	
0 NO VEHICLES USED	0 0.0	2 22.2	6 85.7	6 20.0	8 57.1	22 35.5
100 PLANE ONLY	1 50.0	1 11.1	0 0.0	1 3.3	0 0.0	3 4.8
11000 CAR AND TRAIN	0 0.0	5 55.6	0 0.0	0 0.0	3 21.4	8 12.9
11100 CAR, TRAIN, PLANE	0 0.0	1 11.1	0 0.0	10 33.3	3 21.4	14 22.6
100001 BUS, OTHER	1 50.0	0 0.0	0 0.0	5 16.7	0 0.0	6 9.7
100100 BUS, PLANE	0 0.0	0 0.0	1 14.3	8 26.7	0 0.0	9 14.5
COLUMN TOTAL	2 3.2	9 14.5	7 11.3	30 48.4	14 22.6	62 100.0

CHI-SQUARE = 57,39851 WITH 20 DEGREES OF FREEDOM
NUMBER OF MISSING OBSERVATIONS = 3

When the coding stage is completed, the analyst is faced with a data matrix with as many columns as there are variables and rows as there are cases. His task is to reduce the information contained in thousands of matrix cells to some degree of comprehensible order. This means, in practice, showing how different variables are related to each other. Explanation is achieved by showing how variables influence each other, preferably linking the isolated relationships into chains or networks. Reducing the data matrix is a matter of condensing columns together.

Survey analysis, then, is variable-centred, and in the process all sight is lost of individual cases. Subgroups of cases may, it is true, be retained in the analysis, but a subgroup is defined by common values on certain variables. Subgroups are made up of cases similar to each other, and differing from cases in other subgroups, in respect of selected variables.

ORGANISING A DATA MATRIX FOR ANALYSIS

Let us elaborate the image of a data matrix. As has been suggested, the columns are identified with each variable in the order in which the corresponding questions occur in the questionnaire. Similarly, the rows are probably imagined as numbered in the order in which the questionnaires were completed. The row and column orders are thus determined by the exigencies of the data collection phases. Can we reorder the columns, and perhaps the rows, to help the analytic process?

Regardless of the analytic objective, the variables should be reorganised into blocks of columns in such a way that each block contains only those variables relating to the same time period. Many of the variables will result from questions about the respondents' present attitudes, behaviour and characteristics. Other questions will have probed different periods in his past. Obviously in our search for variables which influence other variables, no variable in a block representing the present can influence a variable in any earlier block period. If, for example, we find that present income is related to the amount of education received, we can eliminate the explanation that present income in any sense causes past education. Equally, we cannot in logic identify one variable as a cause and another as effect if they both are in the same time block. Suppose present income and present ambitions were found to be related, we could not, on this evidence, prefer either explanation that 'income produces ambition' or 'ambition causes high income', even if one explanation were substantively true and the other false.

If the objective of the analysis is to trace the effect of certain

Figure 5 SCHEMATIC REPRESENTATION OF THE ANALYTIC
ORGANISATION OF A DATA-MATRIX

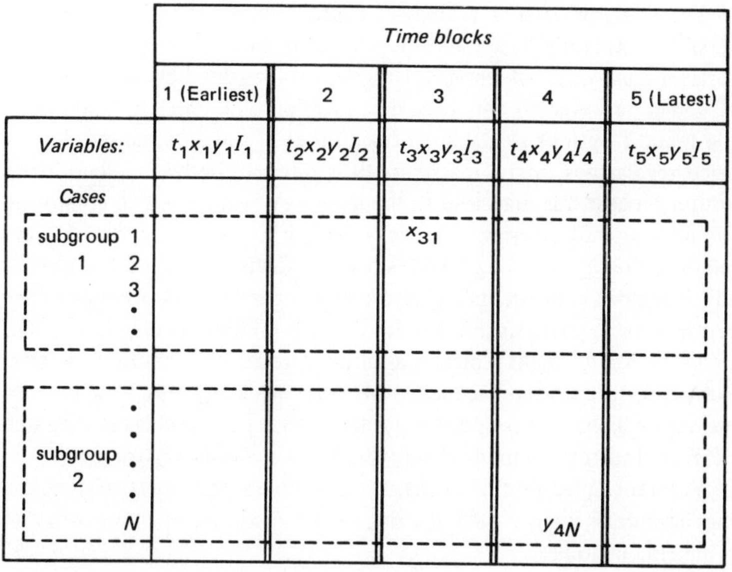

	Time blocks				
	1 (Earliest)	2	3	4	5 (Latest)
Variables:	$t_1 x_1 y_1 I_1$	$t_2 x_2 y_2 I_2$	$t_3 x_3 y_3 I_3$	$t_4 x_4 y_4 I_4$	$t_5 x_5 y_5 I_5$
Cases					
subgroup 1 1 2 3 • •			x_{31}		
• • subgroup • 2 • N				y_{4N}	

patterns of face-sheet or other variables (in other words, if predetermined subgroups exist), the cases can usefully be rearranged into blocks representing the subgroups. Then the central problem in the analysis becomes a question of how far the dependent variables are homogeneous within blocks and heterogeneous between blocks.

Figure 5 shows the organisation of a data matrix for analysis. The raw variables are given lower case letters and a subscript number representing the time block to identify them. The cases are organised into subgroup blocks. The size of each time—and sub—group block depends upon the number of variables and cases they respectively subsume. The reasons for using the letters t, x, y will be discussed in the final chapter; I stands for a composite index drawing upon a number of variables.

The body of the table holds the observed values of each variable; x_{31} represents the value of case 1 on variable x_3, y_{4N} the value of case N on variable y_4. By definition, all cases within a subgroup have comparable values on one or more variables; different subgroups hold different values on those variables.

The strategy of survey analysis centres upon the linkages between variables. Analysis based on subgroups of cases is a special case of variable analysis in which each subgroup is identified by a common set of values on selected variables. The logic of time imposes limits upon the tactical options available to trace order in the data matrix. We can trace regularities in the matrix both within and between time blocks. Within blocks, this may lead to the merging of variables into composite variables or indices; between blocks, we try to unravel cause-and-effect relationships by deciding which observed relationships are meaningful and which are coincidental. Then we may proceed to ask what gives rise to meaningful relationships, and under what conditions they hold good. Links between blocks which can be interpreted meaningfully, because they form a patterned sequence in time, are analogous to a tune or melody in music. Correspondingly, the merging of variables at the same point in time into an index is comparable to a chord or harmony.

The remainder of this chapter is concerned with ways of distilling the harmonies in the data matrix; in the next, we examine ways of producing melodies.

ESTABLISHING THE MEANING OF VARIABLES

Survey interviews and questionnaires are attempts to conduct question and answer sessions between the researcher and many respondents. The questions vary as little as possible between respondents, and their answers to each one are treated as variables. But these variables do not necessarily mean what they appear to say, in at least two senses. When an interviewer asks a standardised question, we cannot know, however hard we may try to ensure it, whether its meaning is unambiguously received and responded to by the respondents. To the extent that it is variously interpreted, so is the meaning of the responses in doubt. Further reinterpretation may occur in the coding process, when third persons acting as coders or interviewers may be involved in fitting a response into one of a limited number of alternatives. Thus the situation has become very different from an ordinary interaction. One actor (literally an actor, for he is mouthing the words of the questionnaire designer) asks another man's question; he either notes what he considers the gist of the answer for yet another to classify into a category set, or himself encodes the answer into a prescribed set of alternatives. In neither case is any clarification of the respondent's meaning feasible.

This is not the place to consider the controversies of interviewing methods; suffice it to note that a considerable amount of encoding and decoding has entered the communication between question and coded answer and that some distortion of meaning is likely in the process. Thus it is inherent in the nature of the method of data collection to make the meaning of a variable problematic.

The second way in which the meaning of a variable can alter occurs when the analyst treats the data as coded as indicating some more general concept than the variable itself. With the exception of age and sex, almost every variable in a survey is really a sample from a conceptual universe. The concept might be an attitude, a way of behaving, social class, morale or the cost of living. Whatever the subject matter of the survey or the factors examined as causes, concomitants or consequences of the subject-matter, each factor will usually be a concept which cannot be directly measured or assessed. Instead, the strategy is to find variables or attitudes to represent the concept, in the same way that the units in a survey are usually individuals chosen as examples of a larger population. But the analogy is with *quota*, not random, *sampling*, because there is no universe of items which can be used as a sampling frame. Although justifying arguments and evidence are produced, the interpretation of the data as an indicator of a particular concept is, in the last resort, a matter of judgment.

Arguing validity

Thus a variable has a meaning which cannot be separated from the context of its analysis. If we asked classes of students whether they hoped to undertake postgraduate training, the responses might be used as indications of many different concepts—academic aspirations, a desire to avoid job seeking, or the realism of their hopes. Sometimes, an individual response may be used as an indicator of a quality which has little to do with its apparent content, as when a mother's responses about how she handles her children are coded by the degree of discretion her strategy allows to the child.[1] The analyst, like Alice in Wonderland, may choose to regard a variable as meaning what he wants it to mean, but he must take great care to convince the sceptic.

If we see all data as symptoms of a position on a concept which cannot itself be measured or assessed, we cannot avoid asking how adequately the indicator represents the concept. This, of course, is the familiar problem of validity. Equally, if we are relying on a very small number of indicators of a single concept, the sampling-from-a-universe-of-items perspective will alert us to the risks inherent in small samples, the problem of reliability. Finally, if the concept is to be assessed by combining variables into an index (thus strengthening the stability of the concept), how are candidate variables to be selected and weighted?

Much of the rationale for the concepts of validity and reliability derives, not from social research, but from psychometrics—the measurement of psychological qualities like intelligence or authoritarianism. Unlike most social research, psychometric tests are usually concerned with decisions about individuals. Is A or B better suited to this job? What kind of training should C be advised to undertake? In these situations, errors are costly in both human and financial terms. To reduce errors, enormous resources have gone into developing and evaluating these tests. Typically they will be quite lengthy, resulting in a total score constructed from dozens of items.

In social research there is not the same need for precision, nor for so accurate a classification of individuals. If less reliability results, the outcome may simply be to lower an observed correlation rather than nullify it. With fewer items comprising each index, more variables can be covered in a limited interview or questionnaire.[2] Finally, the more varied or monotonous the items, the less cooperation can be expected from each respondent. For these reasons, complex indices are less likely to be used in survey analysis.

The simplest form of index relies on only one indicator, its validity being justified primarily by its content. If the question and the concept it represents make sense, the burden of disproving its validity lies with the sceptic. Failing falsification, the variable is said to have *logical* validity.

Sometimes a single variable is used as the indicator of a concept in a less direct, and perhaps more questionable, manner. In Britain the Registrar-General's *Classification of Occupations* is often used as an index of social class. Almost any job, given sufficient description, can be reliably classified into one of five social class groups using the Registrar-General's detailed classification of over 30,000 jobs. While the reliability of the variable so obtained is high because the classification is so comprehensive, one may query its validity. Is social class really reducible to a five stage hierarchy or professional, managerial, intermediate, semiskilled and unskilled occupations? Stratification theorists tend to emphasise at least three criterion themes in social class: economic class, social status and power. To serve as an adequate index of class in this composite sense, occupations as classified into these five classes must account for most of the covariation between all three criteria. But if theorists find it useful to isolate three components of the concept, is it likely that a single indicator can adequately represent them all? And if so, then an empirical demonstration of their interrelatedness is, of course, impossible.[3]

The criticism levelled here against using occupation as an index of social class is derived from one of the two rules of thumb for assessing the validity of an indicator: Does it make sense? and Does it work? Both are a matter of judgment, and it must be said for its proponents that an occupational indicator, in some form, is widely used. In Britain, the Hall-Jones scale[4] is an empirically derived occupational hierarchy, and in the United States there are the Edwards system used by the Bureau of the Census and Blau and Duncan's *Index of Occupational Status*.[5] Despite their ambiguity, one may ask whether it makes sense to equate occupational level with social class when what the researcher may well really be interested in is, in fact, the occupational hierarchy?

There is little doubt, though, that in many areas of social life, position in the occupational hierarchy does work in distinguishing between different behaviour and attitude patterns. Many differences in the way mothers say they bring up their children vary systematically according to whether their husbands are in manual or non-manual jobs.[6] The Registrar-General's social class classification is based on its success in explaining natality and mortality rates in the early 1920s.[7] On the other hand, J. W. B. Douglas had to change his index of social class between his two books, *Children under Five* and *Home and School*, reporting on a panel of the same children at different ages.[8] Both books are about the influence of social class on child development, the first concentrating on physical, and the second on educational, development. Having defined social class in terms of the father's occupation in the first volume, he found so much mobility of occupations in the second volume that he redefined class using a more complex index based on the child's *grandfathers'* jobs and its parents' schooling. In doing so he removed an essential characteristic of social class, the possibility that an individual's class position can change in his life history, with corresponding effects on class-related attitudes and behaviour.

Both the Newsons and Douglas produce findings which show that what they label social class does work in discriminating between classes on other variables. Their indicators have, therefore, some *pragmatic* validity and, to the extent that they discriminate in ways which would be theoretically expected, they have *construct* validity. If they had more *logical* validity one would expect these two kinds of working validity to increase. Instead, it might be said that the demonstrations of working validities have obscured our understanding of what social class really is, instead of aiding our understanding by demonstrating some consequences of one of its components.

Logical validity, the requirement that it should make sense to interpret a variable as an indicator of a concept, is thus a necessary condition to bridge the gap between indicator and concept. The requirement is strengthened if we insist that 'making sense' does not mean simply any plausible rationale, but the *most* plausible. It is plausible to use occupational level as direct indicator of social class, but it is more plausible to interpret occupation in terms of a position in an occupational hierarchy, which itself may well be a component of social class.

INDEX CONSTRUCTION

Supposing then that, dissatisfied with relying on a single indicator, one wishes to construct an index combining a number of variables. At its simplest, the index values may be assigned by fiat to certain combinations of variables, subject of course to the index 'making sense' as a measure of the intended concept. For example, the writer obtained information on the educational level of both parents of East African schoolboys, and wished to classify the pupils according to the educational level of his home. Since very few parents had received more than primary schooling, and most had never been to any school, it seemed meaningful to construct a home literacy index on the basis of whether both, one, or neither parent had ever attended school. In this case, two literate parents were deemed to make a home more literate than one, even though the one might have been a graduate, and the two only primary school leavers.

A more complicated index was necessary to assess the educational commitment of the pupil's family, based upon the extent to which the pupil's school age brothers and sisters had attended school. If schooling had been compulsory, the index might have been simply the ratio of years in school after the leaving age to the total number of years up to the age of twenty put in by the family. For example, a family with one elder sibling aged eighteen and still at school would have scored $2:2 = 1.0$ (meaning two years in school out of two years eligible), while a family with a seventeen-year-old still at school and a twenty-four-year-old who had left at sixteen would score $1:(1 + 4) = 0.20$. In East Africa there is no compulsory schooling, and therefore no compulsory age for entry nor a minimum leaving age. This means that late schooling occurs as well as no schooling. In this index, the total number of years' schooling obtained by all siblings was divided by the total ages over six (the minimum starting age) and up to a maximum of twenty-one, this being taken as the range of years within which schooling might occur. Pupils without sibs of school age or over were excluded from the index calculation because they would have appeared to have the highest possible value ($0:0 = 1.0$) when no other schooling could have occurred.

This again is a relatively simple arithmetic index, made possible because years of schooling, number of siblings and their ages were all metric level measures. It is therefore legitimate to add, divide, and base the index on a form of average.

But it did not include a further component which was judged to be of great importance in the family's commitment to education. This was based on local factors—that girls have much less chance of education than boys, and that entry into post-primary schools and colleges is a scarce resource, not available to all on demand. Perhaps, then, girls getting education should be given more weight than boys, and higher levels of education should be given more weight than lower levels? Weighting the components of an index is a frequent practice, usually carried out by one of two methods, the distributional or the analytic.

The *distributional method of weighting* involves weights calculated from relevant frequencies obtained either from the sample data itself or from population parameters. In the East African example, we could have taken population parameters from the national education statistics, finding out what proportion of boys and girls separately enter the primary, secondary and tertiary levels of education. For boys, the numbers per thousand were roughly 700, 88 and 18 respectively. These figures cannot be used directly as weights because they would give the least weight to those with post-secondary education and most to those with primary only. If, however, we take the reciprocal of each, and then divide each reciprocal by the lowest (the primary school weight), we arrive at weightings of 1 for primary schooling, 8 for secondary schooling and 39 for tertiary, thus allowing the construction of an index which takes account of the relative difficulty of getting into each stage of education. The family's score is now the weighted number of years' schooling obtained divided by the total number of school age years in the family.

There are obvious imperfections in the index, such as the weighting assumption that dropping out only occurs at the end of each stage of schooling, rather than at any point, or that it was equally difficult to get into the next stage whether the attempt was recent or more distant (since there has been a considerable expansion of all levels of education over the past decade). Nevertheless, the relative weights are considerable, suggesting that weighting was both necessary and insensitive to minor imperfections.

Suppose, though, that we had no external criterion, like the relative difficulties of obtaining each stage of education. Could weightings have been derived from an analysis of the proposed components of the index? We shall give two examples of *analytic weightings* of social class indicators to show alternative methods. The first introduces the technique of multiple regression, and the second of factor analysis.

To follow the first method we must say a word about *multiple regression*. Its aim is to estimate the value of one (dependent) variable given the value of other, related variables. The technique, at first sight paradoxically, requires that we know the values of the dependent variable before we set out to estimate it. The point, however, is to see how effectively we could use our knowledge of other measured variables to reproduce the dependent variable. If it can be shown that a satisfactory close estimate (or prediction) has been made, the method can then be applied to other samples in which it is impractical to correct evidence on the dependent variable, but practical to do so on the predictor variables.

The multiple regression equation provides the best estimate* of how

*It is 'best' in the sense that no other method would, given the same data, reduce the amount of error in the estimate by as much, this amount being measured by the squared deviations of the actual values from their estimated values.

much each predictor variable contributes to the variations in the dependent variable. Each of these weights is a measure of the effect of one variable on the dependent variable, other things being equal; the 'other things' being the other variables taken into account in the equation.

Let us suppose, to take an example which will recur in the next chapter, that we have measures of family status, school reputation, and degree of ambition for a sample of schoolboys. We are concerned to see how much of the variety of degrees of ambition can be accounted for by family status and school reputation, taking into account the fact that family and school status are correlated. If we call family status X_1, school reputation X_2, ambition X_3, we can set up the multiple regression equation

$$X_3 = bX_1 + cX_2 + a$$

which means: 'Measured ambition can best be estimated as the sum of family status weighted by b units, plus c units of school reputation, plus a constant factor.' This final factor is the value of X_3 if X_1, and X_2 both had weights of zero (i.e. if neither of these factors contributed to measured ambition). It is an artifact of the particular units of measurements, and can be eliminated if necessary (see page 117). Normally, we would not wish to eliminate it when the weightings are to be used on a later sample to provide estimates of a variable which we will not be in a position to measure directly.

Hollingshead and Redlich were concerned to trace the way social class affects the incidence and treatment of mental disorder.[9] To do so they needed an index of social position which, they reasoned, could be based on the same commonly accepted symbolic characteristics as determines status positions in the community. A random sample of 552 households in the community being studied provided detailed data on 'the size of the family, its participation in economic, religious, educational and leisure-time institutions as well as members' values, attitudes, aspirations, standards of living, ideas of the future and their frustrations, desires, hopes and fears'. Using both information supplied by the respondents and the interviewer's own impressions, these sociologists classified each family into one of five social class levels.

They agreed on 96 per cent of the families independently, and minor disagreements on the remaining 4 per cent were settled jointly. Although it turned out that they had used rather different criteria, they agreed that the main considerations were where a family lived, how it made its living, and its tastes, cultural leanings and use of leisure time. They concluded that the best corresponding indicators were address, the head of household's job and, to indicate the general area of taste, culture and leisure, the level of full-time education the head of the household had received.

The task now was to find the weighted combination of these three items which best predicted the class position agreed upon for each member of this sample. Given such an index, it could then be applied to a different sample to explore the mental disorder correlates of class. Previous ecological research in the area had resulted in a six point scale for classifying any address from 'the finest homes to the poorest tenements', which was used to evaluate addresses. Occupations were rated on a seven-point scale based upon the United States Census prestige classification of socio-economic groupings. The educational level was also assessed on a seven-point scale ranging from a graduate degree to less than seven years in school.

Next all families were scored on these variables, giving a score pattern of four items, including the previously judged class position. Ranking these patterns from high (1,1,1,1) to low (5,6,7,7) revealed the natural groupings, the more frequent, and the missing status inconsistencies, but it still left unsolved the problem of how judged class position could best be derived from the three indicators. By calculating the multiple regression of the three onto judged class, weights of approximately 6 for residential area, 5 for the education, and 9 for the occupation of the head of the household were obtained. Ignoring the constant factor in the equation, this produced a continuum of status scores from 20 to 134. Finally, the cutting point in this continuum, to restore the index to a 1 to 5 scale was determined by comparing the raw scores with the weighted scores. 'Where there was homogeneity in the patterns of raw scale scores, and congruity of these scores with judged class position, we assumed that the cluster was indicative of a functional segment of the community's status system. Where there was heterogeneity in the score clusters, we assumed there was indeterminacy in the status system',[10] and the areas of greatest heterogeneity provided the cutting points.

This is a sophisticated index involving a considerable effort in its construction, but resulting in a scoring procedure which is easy to apply to new cases. It makes sense, if one can accept that social position in the vertical hierarchy of this community is based on an evaluation of the home, the way a family makes its living, and its tastes, because the relative significance of each factor is distilled from the data itself. It reproduces the agreed ratings of two sociologists who had worked closely in the community on the local stratification system. Whether it succeeds in its attempt to reproduce 'the socially discriminating comparisons people make of each other in their day-to-day behaviour'[11] depends on whether we believe that the sociologists' judgments achieved this. The validity of the index is not established empirically, even though the high degree of agreement between the sociologists is an encouraging sign of reliability.

Another index in the general area of social class illustrates the use of *factor analysis* for index construction and how the particular aims of an enquiry may preclude the use of existing indices. Social class is the independent variable in the work of the research team led by Basil Bernstein. Like the previous example the specific meaning of social class in this research was also family social status. The sample used was deliberately skewed towards working-class children, and therefore the index used had to be sensitive to fairly precise differences within working and lower middle groups. Brandis, who describes the index construction,[12] also wished to improve the reliability of the index by including more than just father's occupational status. Without much discussion of the reasons for his choice, the author decided that the components should be father's occupational status as measured by the rating of his present or most recent job in the Hall-Jones scale, the mother's occupational status as measured by the Hall-Jones scaling of her highest-ever job (mothers of young children being more likely to put financial or domestic reasons first for their most recent job), and the educational status of each parent. Inspection of the educational level frequencies showed that two thirds of both parents were in the lowest category, and so, to avoid an unduly skewed distribution, education was rated simply in terms of whether or not the parent had more than the minimal legal level. Treating all variables as though they were interval level measurements, the correlations between them all were factor analysed, using the principal components method.

MULTIPLE REGRESSION AND FACTOR ANALYSIS

Like multiple regression techniques, factor analysis is a method of examining the relationships between a number of variables. Both methods assume that the relations between variables are *linear*, meaning that there is the same relationship between two variables at any section of the range of values. A scatter diagram plotting all cases on both variables could be summarised by drawing a straight line through the

Fig. 6 SCHEMATIC REPRESENTATION OF MULTIPLE REGRESSION AND FACTOR ANALYSIS

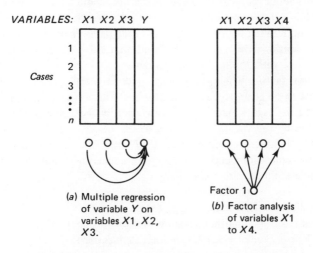

Source: From *Introduction to Multivariate Analysis for the Social Sciences* by John P. Van de Geer. W. H. Freeman and Company. Copyright © 1971.

85

cloud of points. Even this assumption is not as restricting as it may sound, for many curves can be transformed to linear relationships by, for example, converting raw values to their logarithmic equivalents.

Where the two techniques differ basically is that factor analysis reveals groupings, or clusters of variables which in turn may permit one to reduce the data from a series of measurements on a number of variables to a smaller number of dimensions. In regression analysis, one asks what combination of known variables would provide the best estimate of the values of a dependent variable if, in subsequent applications to a similar population, the dependent value were unknown. We can visualise the difference by referring to the simplified versions of Fig. 5 shown in Fig. 6.

Ignoring the time-blocks, the arrows indicate in (a) how variables 1, 2, and 3 are used to estimate variable Y in the multiple regression technique, and in (b) how a new 'unobserved' variable, a factor, is inferred from four observed variables. Hollingshead and Redlich asked how they could best predict judged class position from knowledge of a family's residence, and the head of the household's job and education. Bernstein's team, by contrast, asked whether there was a common factor underlying the four variables of each parent's occupational status and educational history. They found that 66 per cent of the total amount of variation in the four variables could be accounted for by a common factor, which they identified as social class. The relative weights to be given to each indicator are reduced to a common unit by dividing the factor loading (the correlation between the factor and the variable) by the standard deviation of the variable, resulting in weights of 0.51 (father's occupation), 0.57 (mother's occupation), 1.75 (father's education) and 1.74 (mother's education). Rounding crudely to whole numbers, this meant that;

Social class = (Hall-Jones rating of father's job) +
  index   (HJ mother's highest ever job) + 3 (father's
               education) + 3 (mother's education).

Finally, the total index was compressed into seven categories, the names of which indicate the sensitivity of the scale, the marginal and mixed categories containing families where there were discrepancies between the class indicated by parent's job and/or education. Thus:

'pure'	predomin- antly	marginally	mixed class	marginally	predom- inantly	'pure'

middle class   working class

PRINCIPAL COMPONENT ANALYSIS

A word on the principal components method of factor analysis. Factor analysis is a general term for a variety of methods for seeking hidden or underlying structures in a data matrix. One of the major choices to be made before starting is whether the variables are to be regarded as totally, or only partially, reliable indicators of the concept embodied in their name. We may be confident in saying that our information on when a person left school is a reliable measure of when that person left school, in a sense in which we would not have such confidence that a person's mark in a mathematics examination was a reliable assessment of his mathematical skills. In the former case, we assume that the method used to obtain the information did not affect the quality of the information obtained, while in the latter case we admit that other methods of assessment might well result in different (but still related) results. In factor analysis unreliability due to measurement error is taken into account; in principal component analysis any such error is ignored. Now, the first stage in a factor analysis is to produce a correlation matrix of all variables, in which the principal diagonal holds the correlations of each variable with itself. This value will be 1 if it is calculated mechanically, but when the variable is in some degree unreliable, a value of 1.0 would be misleading. If we have a better estimate of a variable's reliability (perhaps obtained empirically) that figure can, and should, be used in the diagonal. The result is to change the analysis from one giving the principal components to one giving an estimate of a factor structure. Thus, where the variables are reliable by definition, the diagonal elements are unity, and a *principal components* analysis results. Where the variables are treated as imperfectly reliable indicators, the diagonal elements are less than unity, and the resultant analysis is of the *classical factor* or *common factor* type. A principal component analysis will eventually account for all the variance in the data matrix, producing as many principal component factors as there are variables in the process, all of which will be unrelated (uncorrelated or orthogonal) to each other. It is only a data reduction exercise when most of the variance is accounted for by the earliest appearing factors, and the analyst ignores the later factors.

In classical factor analysis the aim is to find some underlying regularity or structure in the data. This structure is determined by what the different variables have in common, each variable being conceived of as partially determined by common or shared variance, and partly by variance unique to itself. By definition, unique variance cannot be subsumed by a factor nor related to any common factor. Variance which remains unaccounted for by the factors extracted includes an element of error in measurement. Classical factor analysis is the major analytical tool in the field of psychometrics, and has resulted in many indices of psychological qualities, the best known examples of which are intelligence tests. Most general intelligence tests are constructed and validated on the basis of those factors of mental abilities which factor analysis has isolated.

In survey research both common factor analysis and principal components analysis are used frequently to handle attitude data. A typical example can be seen in the Plowden Report's national survey of parents of primary school children, which isolated fourteen dimensions of attitudes from eighty variables.[13] These dimensions are then used as a more economical and more reliable index of attitudes than the individual items from which they were created. The scaling of attitudes has received a great deal of attention from social psychologists, who have construed a variety of methods: Thurstone, Likert, social distance, semantic differential, Guttman, and so on. They all aim to determine whether a set of items can be treated as measuring a single conceptual dimension. Their underlying assumptions and their advantages vary; the interested reader is referred to one of the many texts[14]—and a computer.

VARIABLE CROSS-CHECKING FOR MEANING

Finally, while we are considering the ways in which the data matrix can be squeezed into fewer and more reliable substantive variables, we should not neglect the process of variable editing. Just as individual cases must be edited for inconsistencies, such as teenage widows or gross income less than net income, so variables can be cross-checked as a further clue to their meaning. If a professed interest in sport was negatively related to taking part in sport, watching it, and discussing it, one would have good cause to be worried about the meaning of one or all of these variables; examining all their interrelationships would probably indicate which had gone awry.

As an example, consider the attempt to measure job satisfaction in the first report of the General Household Survey.[15] The authors admit that a single question on what people think of their present job, with permitted answers ranging from 'very satisfied' to 'very dissatisfied' may be inadequate, and confess their preference for a multidimensional approach covering such different components of job satisfaction as pay, conditions, hours, expectations, etc. Even though nine out of ten people said they were very or fairly satisfied (suggesting that it would be naive to take answers entirely at their face value), the proportions who intended to change their jobs increased from 5 per cent of the 'very satisfied' to 59 per cent of the 'very dissatisfied'. Furthermore, taking those respondents who admitted to some degree of dissatisfaction (48 per cent) all the main reasons for dissatisfaction were found to be increasingly related to the degree of dissatisfaction. As these are the kinds of relationships one would expect from a measure of dissatisfaction, the question has some construct validity.

> *'Fact' is an emotive word, compounded of perception, observation
> and interpretation.* HERMAN BONDI

We all know that facts do *not* speak for themselves. Statistical facts, despite all the attention which is paid to objectivity in their collection, are no exception, whether they are figures showing the incidence of, or the relationships between, phenomena. As we have seen in chapter 3, relationships between pairs of variables, while they may answer some relatively superficial questions, also pose more difficult questions. In chapter 4, we discussed the analysis of configurations of variables, in which the time order of the variables was either irrelevant or unknown. In this chapter we are concerned to answer predominantly why? questions about relationships. Why is it that the more fire engines attending a fire, the more damage is caused? Why is achievement at school so often related to the pupil's father's job? What conditions affect the success of a publicity campaign? Why is there a low correlation between occupational status and earnings?

These are all, in a general sense, questions about causes and consequences. Causal analysis of empirical data is not fully accepted in the British survey movement, partly because of philosophical objections to the notion of causality, and partly because most survey organisations have been content to describe population subgroups and correlated variables without risking an explanation which might subsequently be shown as false. So it is necessary to start with a few observations about the notion of causation.

CAUSAL EXPLANATIONS AND SOCIAL SURVEYS

It is undeniable that logically we can never be sure that A is the cause of B. In every known instance of A, B might also have happened, and we may feel confident that B will continue to happen after every instance of A. But this is not enough to establish that A causes B. Our confidence is only based on a notion of probability. We may have a very plausible explanatory theory of why B is linked to A, but in that case the idea of causality has been imported with a theory, and a theory can be disproved but never proved. It becomes increasingly plausible as it makes sense of an increasing variety of observations and situations. If it is contradicted by an event, it is logically false and must either be modified accordingly or totally rejected.

The task of science is to explain past observations by linking them in a theoretical 'cause-and-effect' chain. The theory, to be of any real usefulness, must lead to predictions about future observations which can be tested and, perhaps, falsified. If it survives testing, it gains credence but is not thereby verified. It is therefore inherent in a scientific theory to live dangerously. The truth of a cause and effect relationship is not an absolute; the scientist moves haltingly towards it, but never arrives at it.

In social science it is very rare to find a situation in which A is invariably followed by B. Much more likely are imperfect correlations, leading to conclusions couched more specifically in probabilistic terms than other sciences may use: 'a high proportion of B's were also A's'. Survey research cannot mirror the ideal experimental situation in which all the factors that might cause a particular effect are controlled except for one independent variable. In an experiment, if the dependent variable changes in line with the independent causal one, then we can conclude that the latter influences the former. Instead, surveys have to rely on methods of statistical control to tease out, or control, the effects of other variables besides the independent one. Only those variables which have been measured in the survey are eligible for statistical control and there are frequently difficulties which make such control impossible in practice. In an experiment, uncontrolled variables lose their biasing influence when cases are randomly allotted to an experimental or a control group. Survey research cannot rely on the random selection of subjects to diminish the effects of uncontrolled factors, since with *ad hoc* sampling frames, non-contacts and refusals, biases of varying degrees may have crept into the most rigorous random sampling procedure.

Thus the surveyor is left prey to a variety of uncertainties. Causality is of dubious logical status, the variables to be explained are subject to multiple influences and hence only partial explanations can be expected, random sampling introduces margins of error and confidence limits, and unmeasured variables may be exerting unknown influences.

This has led to a tradition of caution among surveyors who have often shied away from testing the explanations they suggest, either implicitly or explicitly, in interpreting their findings. After a 'factual' account of the methods used, research reports may be limited to commentaries between the tables (often simply translating them into words), and perhaps speculations on why two variables are related in an observed way, or a caution about small bases for percentages. A typical example occurs in the *General Household Survey* which cautions against comparing 'white' and 'coloured' respondents on the grounds of 'the possibility [of] demographic differences between the two groups which explain differences in other areas of comparison; for example, any difference between their age distributions is very important because age is closely associated with many other variables'.[1] Except as regards housing, the *General Household Survey* accordingly ignores the 'coloured' population when it could have offered some evidence on, for example, how much being 'coloured' affects one's employment (by comparing 'white' and 'coloured' subgroups of the same age and education).

The cautious approach means, as Trow has pointed out, trying hard 'not to be wrong in what [is said], and the way not to be "wrong" (i.e. vulnerable to criticism) is (*a*) to pay very great attention to the techniques of sample design and data collection, and (*b*) to say little beyond what the data show directly'.[2] The result is to throw the baby out with the bathwater. Whatever the philosophical status of causation, those who commission, those who conduct, and those who read research are interested in finding out the causes and effects of a situation in a commonsense sense. Even a distinguished philosopher of science has to use cause and effect terminology to explain the decline of causality in science: "The causal principle fell into disrepute during the first half of our century as an *effect* of two independently acting *causes:*

the criticisms of empiricist philosophers and the growing use in science and technology of statistical ideas and methods" (italics added).[3]

The question, then, is who will make the connections, provisional and uncertain as they may be, between causal factors and their consequences? Should it be left to the reader, who cannot get at such evidence as exists and whose guesses will consequently be highly speculative? It would seem preferable that the analyst should pursue his hunches, conjectures, and insights through the data, publishing the evidence for (and against) his interpretations. Someone is likely to infer a causal connection in the data, however 'neutrally' it is presented. The Belgian psychologist, Michotte, suggests that the process by which we arrive at a causal interpretation of events is a natural one, linked with the direct, subconscious process of perception. We do not perceive first and then infer a causal interpretation consciously and logically.

(It is important to recognise that speculations unsupported by evidence can play a valuable part in a survey report, but their conjectural nature should be made explicit. This explicitness will necessarily remind the analyst to substantiate or refute his speculations wherever possible. As three leading social statisticians make clear in a critical evaluation of the Kinsey Report, "unsubstantiated assertions are not in themselves inappropriate in a scientific study. In any complex field where many questions remain unresolved, the accumulated insight of an experienced worker may well be worth putting on record although no documentation can be given".)[4]

We have seen that, in science, how we explain our findings is always a more or less tentative theory, the degree depending on the range and breadth of the evidence it explains or is consistent with. It is not being scientific, then, to refuse to produce theory grounded in the data for reasons of caution. Trow points out that a bolder approach in survey analysis could have a beneficial effect on future research.

Where there is considerable tolerance for the reporting of highly provisional findings and interpretations, there is more likely to be a healthy scepticism and mistrust on the part of the reader, a state of mind much more likely to lead to replications and further related research aiming to see if the findings are in fact as reported, under what conditions they obtain, and so on.[5]

Let us accept the intuitive appeal of cause and effect thinking and make it our objective to demonstrate plausible causal relationships, measuring their magnitude wherever possible. For our purposes, X 'causes' Y if three conditions are met: (*a*) X happens before Y, (*b*) a change in X is likely to be followed by a change in Y, and (*c*) no other variable in the data set can plausibly be shown to be the common cause of the observed fact that Y changes when X changes. There is a fourth condition of some importance, which we shall assume is fulfilled, which is that the relationship can be shown to be statistically significant. Generally, the first explanation to be tested is that 'chance' accounts for an observed relationship. If it does, there is no point in searching for causes.

We shall use 'cause' where others prefer more neutral terms like 'influence', 'generate', and 'produce'. It is a shorthand way of drawing attention to the direction of a relationship: which variable is currently being regarded as the independent and which the dependent variable.

Sometimes, both directions may be examined, where the relationship could be regarded as reciprocal, or where there are no grounds for assuming that one variable precedes the other. The *General Household Survey*, for example, relates the composition of households to the type of tenure by which the house was held.[6] Since it might be argued that a family's housing needs are determined by its composition, one table shows the percentage distribution of types of tenure among households of different composition. This perspective is strengthened by the finding that only one in twelve small younger families owned their house outright compared with nearly half the small older families. But equally it might be argued that house tenure reflects a family's resources and thus determines what kind of family they have: a second table therefore shows the composition of household among different kinds of tenure revealing that mortgage payers are predominantly smaller households, while council house tenants are more evenly spread across the whole spectrum of household types.

In using the terms 'causal' or 'determining', then, the analyst is not so much asserting that one variable actually causes another, as posing the question that it may be, and inspecting the evidence for this possibility. As a data interrogator, he may provisionally accept that the evidence points towards one or other conclusion, but always with the twin provisos in mind of plausibility and 'other things being equal'. Wherever possible he will ask himself what other variables might cause both the observed ones to change. When the variable suggested by an alternative explanation has been measured, he examines whether the observed relationship still holds when the test variable is controlled. 'Controlling for' is a crucial phrase in the analyst's stock of jargon, and simply means that the test variable is the 'other thing being equal'. For example, the reason why the greater the number of fire-engines at a fire (the independent variable, X), the more damage is caused by the fire (dependent variable Y) is not because X and Y are causally related, but because the size of the fire (the test variable, T) determines both. If we examined the XY relationship for big fires and small fires separately, we would find (other things again being equal, such as the availability of fire engines or the proximity of high-risk property) that the XY relationship would come close to disappearing in the subgroups of big and small fires. When the XY relationship among fires of equal size is examined, the original relationship has vanished. It has been shown to be *spurious* or *explained away*.

ELABORATING RELATIONSHIPS

This process of re-examining a relationship between two variables in the light of a third lies at the heart of *tabular* survey analysis. Technically known as elaboration, it is a process, rather than a mechanical procedure, by which it is hoped to clarify a given relationship. Each step is determined by the results of earlier steps and the analyst's own developing vision of the data. Thus there can be no 'right' procedure for a given data set; the product results from the way the analyst chooses to interact with the data.

Explanation
The first step in introducing a third variable into the picture is likely to be taken to help decide whether the relationship is meaningful, and not the result of an *extraneous* variable. As with all steps in elaboration, we choose a test variable on the basis of a hypothesis which, if true, would

95

provide a plausible explanation connecting the hypothesised cause with the two variables in the observed relationship.

It may be helpful at this stage to visualise the hypotheses diagrammatically. In Fig. 7 three variables are shown linked in two ways. Y is the dependent variable whose variation is to be accounted for, X is the independent variable which is associated with Y, and T is the test variable introduced to try to explain the relationship between X and Y. One-way arrows show the causal direction, two-way arrows (not shown) would represent an unknown or reciprocal direction, and the absence of an arrow between two variables shows that their association is not part of the explanation proposed and embodied in the model.

Fig. 7 EXPLANATION AND INTERPRETATION

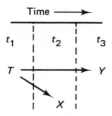

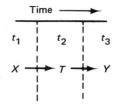

(a) T explains the 'spurious' relationship between X and Y.

(b) T interprets the link between X and Y by adding a link in the causal chain.

In making sense of an independent-dependent variable relationship, the position of the test factor in time is crucial. Fig. 7(a) shows a situation in which the test factor precedes both variables, and in Fig. 7(b) it occurs between X and Y. In both diagrams X must precede Y by definition and, in general, one-way arrows cannot point in any left-leaning direction, for this would mean that a variable was influencing another which had already occurred.

Referring back to Fig. 5 in the previous chapter, it becomes clear why it is useful to classify all variables on a time dimension. The number of different routes through the data the analyst may choose are substantially reduced by the requirement that he must always be travelling in a forward direction.

Both diagrams show alternative causal models, one of which might explain why X is related to Y. They each embody a hypothesis of how the XY relationship can be explained away as 'unreal' (in the sense of having no substantive meaning). Both require the same table to test the hypotheses—a table which shows what happens to the XY relationships when the test variable, T, is controlled.

In order to control a variable, cases are sorted into their component categories, and within each category the relationship between the other two variables is re-examined. Table 10 shows how the relationship between the number of fire engines at a fire (X) and the damage caused (Y) might be explained away, as due to the relationship each variable has with the size of the fire (T). For simplicity, each variable has been dichotomised and their values are represented by a + or − sign.

TABLE 10

Percentage of fires causing serious damage (Y+) by number of fire engines (X) and size of fire (T)

| Size of fire (T) | Number of fire appliances used (X) | | |
	Few (X−)	Many (X+)	Difference
Large (T+)	9%(600)	11%(400)	2%
Small (T−)	29%(400)	32%(900)	3%
	17%(1000)	26%(1300)	9%

Source: hypothetical

Note that Table 10 shows only half the picture by omitting fires causing minor damage $(Y−)$. The omission simplifies the table without losing information because minor damage fires could be deduced by subtracting the percentages from 100 per cent. As always in reading the table, we start with the marginals, and note that XY are related, since serious damage is caused in 26 per cent of fires attended by many appliances, compared with only 17 per cent of fires with a few appliances present, making a 9 per cent difference. But on examining what happens at large and small fires separately, we find that the number of engines attending bears much less relation to the damage caused. The 9 per cent difference is reduced to 2 per cent at large fires and to 3 per cent at small fires. These remaining differences are less important than the size of the decreases. What is significant here is the virtual disappearance of the original relationship when it is examined for separate categories of T, not the small percentage differences which remain. Because we can explain the original relationships in terms of an *antecedent* variable, size of fire, it can be interpreted as *spurious*, and represented as in Fig. 7 (*a*).

Interpretation
Consider another example: suppose it has been observed that older people are more likely to listen to religious broadcasts than younger people (as shown in the bottom line of Table 11). To many analysts, this finding would not be surprising because it fits what they might regard as the 'commonsense' interpretation: as people get older, they come to fear the approach of death more than they did in their younger, more active days; religion comforts those so afflicted, and hence leads to more frequent listening to religious broadcasts. While this sounds plausible enough, we should recognise that it is purely speculation that another variable, 'fear of death', links age to listening behaviour. It is not a finding from the data; it has the status of 'anybody's guess' unless the survey happens to have included this variable and could test the interpretation by introducing it as a test variable. Assuming information on 'fear of death' were not available, is there any way of throwing further light on the hypothesis?

One strategy is to ask oneself what other characteristics are associated with the X and Y variables. Perhaps listening to religious braodcasts is simply a corollary of being an indiscriminating listener who rarely switches off or changes stations. Perhaps listening to religious broadcasts is negatively related to amount of education, since characteristically older people tend to have a lower level of education than the young. If the latter were true, the relationship between age and listening behaviour should be substantially reduced when education is controlled or held equal. Let us assume that the educational level of respondents was available in the data, and examine the effect of holding education constant.

TABLE 11

Percentage of listeners who listen to religious broadcasts (Y+) by age and education

Education (T)	Young (X−)	Age (X) Old (X+)	Difference
High (T+)	9%(600)	11%(400)	2%
Low (T−)	29%(400)	32%(900)	3%
Total	17%(1000)	26%(1300)	9%

Source: Adapted from P. F. Lazarsfeld and M. Rosenberg, eds, *The Language of Social Research* (*Glencoe Free Press*), (1955), p. 117, tables 3 and 4.

In Table 11 education has been presented as a test variable and we find that the relationship again virtually disappears. To interpret: older people are more likely to listen to religious programmes, not because they are old, but because they are less educated and more likely to listen to religious broadcasts. In this case, model (*b*) in Fig. 7 has been elaborated: age (year of birth) precedes education which precedes current listening behaviour. In technical words, age is negatively correlated with education, which is negatively correlated with listening. When the test factor explains the link between *X* and *Y* by successfully invoking an *intervening* variable as the test variable, the result is called *interpretation,* because it shows a link in the causal sequence. It may be, of course, that further links between *X* and *T*, and *T* and *Y* are needed for a fuller understanding of the impact of *X* on *Y*. Neither 'fear of death' nor 'selectiveness of listening' have been tested by the elaboration, but educational level has been introduced as a factor to be taken into account in any theorising.

The alert reader will have noted that Tables 10 and 11 are identical apart from the variable labels. Whether we choose to explain a relationship away as spurious or interpret the effect of a test variable as an intervening link variable depends upon the position of the test variable in the time order. Both show the same pattern of figures: an initial relationship is reduced to a negligible difference when a third variable is held constant. When the test variable precedes the independent variable, the disappearance of the original relationship shows it to have been spurious; when the test variable occurs between the independent and the dependent, the disappearance shows that the test variable forms a link in the causal sequence from independent to dependent.

The first step in interpreting any apparent relationship is to test whether it really exists. Can the relationship be explained away as purely a matter of chance? This is the first plausible explanation we normally test, using a statistical test of significance. If the relationship cannot be explained away as probably a chance result, we then need to consider whether it is spurious, by examining plausible antecedents which may account for the observed result. Here the analyst is using his own judgment of what is plausible and what is not: it is judgments like this which make the interpretation of surveys an individual, non-mechanical affair.

If the relationship cannot be dismissed as spurious, the next step in interpretation is to explore for plausible links between the two variables, to understand better the process or conditions creating the link. Specifically, we would look for any variables which, when held constant, significantly reduce the size of the original relationship.

Although the question of what links occur between two points in a causal chain is obviously crucial to a fuller understanding of the effects of one variable on another, examples of the use of this technique are uncommon in survey research reports. Some writers are inclined to regard this as a failure by analysts to recognise the importance of the method,[7] but it is more likely to be due to the 'one–off' nature of a survey. In designing a survey, one has expectations as to the probable relationships which will be found, and the variables built into the questionnaire will be those seen as the most relevant to the designer's expectations. It is usual to set out to explore the antecedent causes of an expected relationship, whereas intervening variables usually arise from attempts to make sense of the data at the analysis stage. For example, a researcher interested in the general problem of the relationship between social class and educational performance, would design his investigation differently according to whether he was attempting to demonstrate such a link, or to explore its dimensions. If the latter were his aim, he would know beforehand the variables on which he wished to obtain evidence in order to see whether they explain the relationship. His working model would assign social class to the role of the antecedent variable, educational performance as the dependent variable, and his selected variables would be treated, one by one, as independent variables. Intervening variables, on the other hand, only enter the explanatory process as a result of speculative efforts to interpret an unforeseen relationship. Because these relationships are unexpected, it is unlikely that data suitable for testing the explanation suggested by the finding will have been collected in the current survey.

Antecedent variables

Let us examine more closely the nature of an antecedent variable. It is similar in its causal order to the extraneous test variable which explains a two-variable relationship because it precedes both in time. Unlike both an extraneous and an intervening variable, the statistical result of introducing an antecedent variable is that the original relationship is replicated in the three-dimensional table. When this occurs, we have isolated a new factor in the causal sequence, one which influences the independent variable, which in turn influences the dependent.

A moment's thought will make it clear that an antecedent variable will be related to the dependent variable, but that this association should be reduced substantially or disappear if the two are tabulated holding the independent variable constant. Suppose the dependent variable is performance at school, and the causal variable is the amount of interest fathers take in the child's school work. The relationship between these two prompts us to ask what enables fathers to take a lot of interest in their children's work. We test two variables, which happen to be related to each other: social class and whether the father works on night shifts. Controlling for each test variable in turn shows, in both cases, that father's interest and child's performance are still related. Must we stop at this point with the conclusion that the reason why children whose fathers take more interest in their work do better at school could be due either to social class influences or to their own working hours? It may prove possible to choose between these alternatives by tabulating the variables again, this time holding the father's interest constant, and preferring the antecedent variable which loses its relationship to the dependent. In this case, we would prefer the shift work explanation if the data revealed no relationship between shift work and child's performance without the mediating effect of whether father is available to take an interest when homework is done. Social class, however, remains positively related to school performance, whether or not fathers work nights.

Suppressor variables

We have seen that one can err in concluding that a relationship between two variables is real because it is statistically significant, when in fact it is spurious due to the relation of each variable to an antecedent third variable. It is also possible to conclude that a lack of relationship is real when it is in fact due to the suppressing effects of a third variable. Suppressor variables, so called, also may weaken a relationship leading to misleading interpretations.

In a study of trade unionism, Rose found that there was no relationship between the length of time a worker had been a member of a union, and antisemitic attitudes to members of the union's staff. Now, whenever a variable is concerned with a length of time extending over many years, it is always advisable to run the relationship again controlling for age because so many attitudes and behaviour patterns vary with age. On doing so, Rose was able to show that being a member of a union had an effect on this attitude. His data revealed that within each age category, those who had been members of the union longer were less likely to be concerned whether a staff member was Jewish or not. This was because the test factor, age, was positively related to the 'causal' factor, length of union membership, but negatively related to the 'effect' factor, tolerance of Jewish staff members.[8]

As with so many principles of the logic of survey analysis,

Durkheim's *Suicide* provides a clear example of a weak relationship being the result of suppressor conditions. Jews, t will be remembered, are a highly integrated religion in Durkheim's framework, and consequently would be expected to have a lower suicide rate than Gentiles, because suicide rates are associated with low degrees of integration. Noting that this expectation is borne out by the data, he argues that 'the "true" Jewish rate must be even lower than the figures reveal it to be'[9] because Jews are more likely than Gentiles to live under two conditions less conducive to integration, in cities and holding intellectual occupations.

Distorter variables

It is even possible for two variable relationships to lead to interpretations which controlling for a third variable reveals is the opposite of the truth. Again, Durkheim illustrated this clearly. Earlier studies than his own had produced evidence that married people are more likely to commit suicide than the unmarried. By controlling for age, he is able to show that the unmarried have substantially higher rates of suicide than the married within age groupings.[10] Age has a distorting effect because it is positively associated both with marriage and with suicide rates.

Component variables

What is it about married life which reduces the suicide rate? Is it that the kind of people who marry are somehow less predisposed to suicide? Durkheim rejects this argument for a variety of reasons, among them that the 'immunity from suicide' should, on this argument affect husbands and wives equally (which is not the case). Again, 'on the whole, conjugal selection occurs everywhere in the same way, .. [yet] the relative situation of the sexes as to the degree of preservation enjoyed by married persons is not the same in all countries'.[11] If the marriage process acts to select the less suicide-prone, then the comparison of husband and wife rates leads to the conclusion that the same process leads to opposite results in different areas.

Dismissing, therefore, the selection argument Durkheim turns to the marital state itself, and shows that the component in marriage which lowers the suicide rate is the presence of children. Comparing men of

103

similar ages, he shows that widowers with children have lower rates than unmarried men, and that husbands with children have lower rates than husbands without children, who in turn have lower rates than unmarried men. And he conscientiously observes that:

> We have assumed that childless husbands have the same average age as husbands in general, whereas they are certainly younger... If we knew exactly the average age of childless husbands, their aptitude for suicide would surely approach that of unmarried men still more than the ... figures indicate.[1 2]

Thus, Durkheim is able to isolate a component variable, childlessness, of the marital state and show that it is the factor causing the relationship between marital state and the suicide rates. Many of the concepts employed in social science are composites at a fairly high level of generality, such as social class, alienation, age or sex. This makes generalisation using them somewhat unspecific. If we can specify what aspects of these composites are having what effects, the result for social science can only be beneficial.

Specification

A two-variable relationship may not be true for all sorts and conditions of men. If we group cases on a third variable, it may be that the original relationship neither disappears nor is replicated, but varies within each category of the third variable. For example, it has been found that anxiety was greater among boys who had elder brothers or sisters in a grammar school than among boys who had not. When these boys were classified by both their social class and their type of school the relationship between anxiety and having a grammar school sibling virtually disappeared in all groups except among middle-class secondary modern boys, where the level of anxiety was particularly high. In other words, it was possible to specify sets of conditions in which the relationship was enhanced or weakened. The interpretation which the original relationship led to, that the success of an elder sibling places greater pressure on the younger boy which in turn leads to anxiety, has to be modified to fit the data more accurately; that middle-class boys who do less well educationally than their elder siblings suffer much more anxiety than working-class boys in a similar position.

In his effort to understand two variable relationships the analyst must consider the conditions under which its substantive conclusions may vary. When the original is no longer true, the outcome of taking a third variable into account is called *specification* and the relationships which result in the various subgroups are called *conditional relationships*. The purpose of specification is to examine whether the original relationship is constant in a variety of conditions and, if not, to specify the circumstances when the original is changed in the conditionals. This happens whenever the third variable interacts with values of either original variable.

There are many forms of specification, partly because the position in time of the third variable relative to the other two is irrelevant. The important distinction among the different forms is that between those in which the conditional relations reflect the direction, but not the magnitude, of the original and those which do not. In Table 7, for example, we find a two-variable relationship showing that men living in a village were much more likely to work there if they had not been born there than if they were locally born. The data in Table 9 *specify* this relationship, by showing that while the relationship is still true regardless of where their wives were born, it is much stronger among men whose wives were not born locally.

Sometimes the conditional relationships are in different directions, and therefore cannot mirror the direction of the original relationship. Merton, for example, found a small relationship between job satisfaction and participation in local community activities: 41 per cent of those satisfied with their jobs belonging to an organisation compared to 38 per cent of the dissatisfied. But when he examined these two variables controlling for the respondent's felt social class, he found stronger relationships in both groups, but in opposite directions.[13]

Among those who saw themselves as white-collar workers, participation was less likely among those satisfied with their job. Among those who felt that they were working-class, participation was greater among those satisfied with their jobs. In the one instance, participation was negatively related to job satisfaction; in the other, positively. In this

105

TABLE 12

Relationship between job satisfaction and participation in community activities according to class identification

Class identification	Percent who belong to organisations Satisfied with job	Dissatisfied with job
White collar	33% (42)	44% (18)
Working class	44% (118)	36% (99)

example specification resulted in a considerably revised interpretation of the finding.

It is interesting to note that Merton actually concluded from the two-variable relationship that no relationship existed between job satisfaction and participation, because the numbers involved were too small to be statistically significant. Nevertheless this was a relationship he had expected to find, and the spurious non-correlation stimulated the search for an explanation for this lack of relationship. Being able to specify the conditions under which the relationship holds resulted in a better understanding of the links between job satisfaction and participation in local groups.

The uses of specification are legion. To give but two general examples: the degree of interest may specify attitude formation and change; when and/or where a study was made may have a crucial effect on the findings, especially in cross-cultural surveys.

Contextual analysis

Among the many conditions possible, it may be particularly useful to consider as specification variables some factors which incorporate the individual respondent into his social context. In this way we can begin to move away from the atomistic nature of surveys with their tendency to look more like contributions to 'aggregate psychology' than to a social science. To each respondent is attributed, not only his individual responses, but also certain properties derived either from known characteristics of groups, organisations or institutions of which he is a member, or from comparisons between the individuals and other respondents in the same survey. For example, in a study of African schoolboys, the author found it useful to characterise each pupil by whether he was or was not a member of a minority tribe among his fellow pupils; this was information only obtainable after the 'straight counts' of all pupils had identified which were the majority tribes represented. This type of contextual property has been called a *comparative* attribute because it results from a comparison between the respondent and all other members of a sample.

Relational properties are computed from information about the substantive relationship between the respondent and other respondents. In studying school pupils, for example, one might have asked each who their best friend was, or who was the cleverest student in the class. The number of mentions each respondent received from his fellows can then be used to measure his relative popularity or his relative academic esteem. We might, for example, be able to show that pupils from a minority tribe are, by reason of their tribe rather than their personality (however assessed) unlikely to be among the more popular in the school.

Contextual properties are used when members of a collectivity are described (coded) by a characteristic of the group. Davis, for example, studied the members of a number of adult discussion groups and was interested to explain why 'dropping-out' occurred, and particularly how much of the process could be explained by individual characteristics of the members, and how much by characteristics of the groups themselves.[14] He ascribed a variable, the proportion of active members of his group, to each member as a contextual property and used it to specify the relationship between two individual variables, whether a member is active or not, and whether he drops out or not. This analysis reveals two kinds of effects: at the individual (or two-variable) level, more active members are less likely to drop out than the less active; and at the group level, the higher the proportion of active members in a group, the fewer people drop out (although those who do still tend to be the less active). Specification, in this instance, has not only succeeded but has clarified the finding at a sociological, rather than a social psychological, level.

Contextual variables (otherwise variously called 'compositional effects', 'structural effects', or 'climate of opinion') when taken in conjunction with the specification procedure, adds a powerful tool to the survey analyst's collection, and particularly provides

107

a route for sociologists to make better use of surveys.[15]

Types of elaborating variables

We have considered a number of different ways in which stratifying a two-variable relationship by a third, test, variable can elucidate the meaning of relationships, and the stages in a causal sequence. Rosenberg points out that introducing test variables can help in dealing with two problems when interpreting a two-variable relationship.[16] It can help in avoiding false conclusions, and it can help to make our understanding of a two-variable relationship more precise and specific.

False conclusions can be drawn in two ways, by accepting a false interpretation as true, and by rejecting a true interpretation as false. When a relationship is shown to be spurious, the test variable is extraneous to the original interpretation. Demonstrating that a variable is extraneous prevents us accepting a false interpretation. Identifying suppressor variables, by contrast, enables us to avoid rejecting a true interpretation. Distorter variables can, unless recognised, lead to either type of false conclusion: accepting a false hypothesis or rejecting a true one.

Extraneous, suppressor, and distorter variables are third variables introduced to clarify the meaning of a two-variable relationship. With specification, antecedent, intervening, or component variables, our interest moves on to three-variable relationships which cannot be reduced to a set of two-variable relations. Antecedent and intervening variables link three variables in a causal sequence. Component variables and specified relations help make our understanding more precise and specific, especially if contextual variables are used as specifiers.

ALTERNATIVE TO TABLE ANALYSIS

Until recently, tabular analysis seemed to be the only feasible way of imposing some degree of order on the vast amount of information available in a large data matrix. Before the advent of electronic data-processing equipment, the process of creating three or four dimensional tables could be a lengthy one, but it had the advantage of providing results in a form which is relatively easy to understand. The disadvantages of relying on tabular analysis have become much clearer since computers became widely available. Four shortcomings of table analysis are fundamental to the increasing use of multivariate statistical techniques for making sense of large bodies of data.

Analysing data by sorting it into an increasing number of cells means increasingly large samples. The usefulness of a table is roughly determined by the size of its smallest cell. Adding a further dimension to an existing table greatly increases the number of cells available for the same number of cases, the precise increase depending on the number of categories in each variable. For example, a contingency table showing two variables, each taking three values, would have nine cells. Introducing a third variable also with three values would yield a twenty-seven cell table. At this rate, we would rapidly find that many cells were empty or nearly so, particularly as often the extra variables are brought into the analysis because they are thought likely to be associated with earlier variables, and thus, by definition, are not expected to be evenly distributed over all the available cells. It is also unlikely that the variables themselves would be evenly distributed between their component values, causing a further off-balancing factor among the cells.

Even if the distribution of cell frequencies permits viable comparisons, a multicell table still presents more information than the mind can absorb. Psychologists often refer to 'the magic number 7 (± 2)' as indicating the limit of the number of separate items of information the mind can simultaneously manipulate. Thus many-celled tables may not help much in the task of making a data matrix comprehensible.

Tabular analysis, as well as being inefficient in its use of the available data also limits the kind of causal analysis possible to one which, by and large, has to be qualified by the phrase, 'other things being equal'. In order to reduce the number of dimensions in a table and to retain acceptable frequencies in each cell, the analyst frequently finds himself having to ignore variables which are known to contribute to a dependent variable. The variables retained are chosen because they overlap with or contain much of the variation in the omitted variables. For example, in trying to explain the delinquency records of primary school children, social class may be used as an independent variable which contains much of the variation between income and delinquency, and between parental education and delinquency. But the table which results is intrinsically ambiguous in meaning, both because 'social class' is a composite variable including two variables with differing effects of their own, and because there may be yet other kinds of effects when income and education are broadly congruent compared with their separate effects. This latter possibility is called an 'interaction effect', and the more variables known to have separate effects, the many more interaction effects are possible, yet unknown. As Hirschi and Selvin put it,

As long as the number of independent variables included in a table is smaller than the number known to be related to the dependent variable, the meaning of any relation is inherently ambiguous. If poverty, race, education, and overcrowding are all individually related to delinquency, or even if pairs or triples of these variables are studied together, the meaning of any one of these tables must always remain in doubt as long as it is impossible to examine the joint effect of all four independent variables. What appears to be the effect of education and overcrowding is also the effect of race and poverty—and of any other independent variables associated with these four.[17]

Thirdly, and this is a point which is often missed in elaborating two-variable relations, holding a variable constant does not in fact mean that all cases within a category of the controlled variable are equivalent in that respect. Although there is more similarity among them than there is between cases in different categories, the need to limit the number of categories can still mean that a great deal of variation may still exist within categories. 'Controlling for age' simply means removing some of the biggest differences in age, but smaller differences remain, and may in fact account for the relationships we seek to explain. Many nominal variables are derived by imposing a small set of categories upon what is essentially a continuum, and in doing so information is inevitably lost. Tables are inappropriate for restoring or using more sensitive variables.

Finally, there is no clear point at which an analysis based on tables is completed. 'A tabular analyst decide[s] to stop his analysis, . . . more often than not, when he runs out of cases, time, interest or money.' He cannot know whether he has explained all that he can ever explain of his data, 'whether he has explained too little, enough, or indeed whether his overlapping sets of independent variables may have explained the same variation more than once!'[18]

For these reasons, survey analysts are increasingly turning to mathematically more sophisticated techniques to reduce these difficulties. Many of these techniques are only possible because computers are available to make the calculations; this development has led to a frantic elaboration of programs, all too often neglecting basic principles of statistics. It is ironic that this has happened at the same time as a better understanding of the principles of statistical inference has emerged from the significance tests controversy.[19]

This chapter is largely concerned with a strategy of survey analysis in which we seek to identify the causes and consequences of a predetermined dependent variable. We have not suggested a blind approach, in which every variable is related in turn to the dependent variable, for two reasons. It is too prone to the *post hoc* interpretation of a relationship, particularly if the analyst has already become thoroughly familiar with the structure of his data by close inspection. Secondly, statistical significance has no meaning in a blind approach, for how are we to distinguish between the 'real' and the spuriously significant? About 5 per cent of our relations will be significant at the 5 per cent level anyway. And because, in the next stage of introducing third variables as constants to elaborate selected two-variable relations, we are introducing a non-random selection into the procedure, the basic principle that tests of significance are based on departures from random distributions is thereby invalidated.

Nevertheless, the more informed, reasoned selection of relationships to test in a variety of ways which we have advocated, does not eliminate the criticism that the selection is still not made at random. This still means that tests of significance are inappropriate. How then are we to gain confidence in any findings that result?

The only way is by replication of the results on a comparable sample. This may mean dividing randomly the data collected before beginning any analysis, in order to have an exactly comparable data set for replication runs. Or it may be possible to rerun the same analysis on another data set. This will become easier as data banks are more widely used. Confidence in a result comes from finding it repeated in other studies or samples, other than those which gave rise to the hypothesis behind the relationship in the first place.

Data dredging
Mathematical, computer-executed, operations for exploring relationships in a data set are picturesquely known as 'data dredging'. As long as provision is made for a replication sample on which to test the results, some forms of data dredging can be useful tools at the exploratory stage, clearing away the undergrowth for a clearer view of the terrain.

Three types of data dredging have been described as snooping, hunting, and fishing.[20] Fishing is the process of using the data to decide which of a number of possible variables should be included in an explanatory model, compared with snooping as the process of testing all of a predesignated set of hypotheses, and hunting as searching through a data set in order to find some relationships worth testing. Hunting involves no preconceived objectives unlike fishing and snooping. No tests of significance can be meaningfully applied to relationships produced by a hunting expedition.

Fishing 'is often the only way to produce the food needed for the survey analyst's thought'[21] and includes the whole process of elaboration. Besides being necessary in exploratory research, it can also be deceptively attractive with computers to do the hard work. A program known as AID (Automatic Interaction Detector) can carry out a completely systematic fishing trip. The aim is 'to identify and segregate a set of sub-groups which are the best we can find for maximising our ability to predict the dependent variable'.[22] Every variable, and every value of each variable is examined to see how the data can be split into two groups in that way which explains most of the variation in a predesignated dependent variable. Both groups are then subject to the same process, as are the four groups which result. The process continues until no further variation can be explained.

Unfortunately, the results are inherently unstable when the program is repeated on a series of random samples from a data set, because the procedure capitalises on all the variation in the data, including that introduced by random factors. With one set of results bearing little resemblance to another, there is no way of choosing that which best explains the data. The reader should be warned that the program is still widely, and naively, used. It pinpoints precisely the value of replication samples.

If there is a strong case both against restricting ourselves to the relatively simple procedures of table analysis and against using a totally systematic procedure like AID, how can the advances in data processing be used to best advantage? Is there any way of obtaining a picture of what influences what, by how much, and under what varying conditions? The best hope at present seems to lie in path analysis.

It is likely that we shall see an increasing use of path analysis in significant research studies over the next few years. The most recent example is a major attempt to integrate the findings of a variety of studies bearing on the causes of inequality in society. Jencks' finding that 'neither family background, cognitive skills, educational attainment, nor occupational status explains much of the variation in men's incomes' and his evidence for this conclusion, which extends over nearly 400 pages, are summarised by a single path analysis diagram.[23] In a similar vein, the Oxford Social Mobility studies to be published shortly will use path analysis to assess the causes and extent of social mobility since 1949.

Path analysis
Perhaps the main advantage of path analysis is that it imposes on the analyst the necessity to think thoroughly about the implications of an explanatory model he may be developing. As a technique it will not produce a causal explanation from one's data, but it will allow one to test the compatibility of a theoretical explanation with the data to hand. Moreover, the entire model or explanation is tested, rather than a series of hypotheses about two or three variable-relationships in the model, the results of which are difficult to tie together. It 'eliminates a weakness of all previous methods . . . [their] inability

113

to deal with more than one substantive proposition at a time'.[24]

The technique will gain prominence in this country with the publication of the Oxford Social Mobility studies in which it is extensively used to assess the causes of movement between social strata. To illustrate let us look at an example from an article which first drew sociologists' attention to the technique.[25] Duncan takes a study of school pupils' ambitions, and abstracts from the author's text what appears to be his account of how class values are influenced by four variables, ambition, intelligence, the pupil's background, and the socio-economic standing of the school. This account is not spelled out specifically, as we can see from Duncan's selection of relevant statements.

At one point he states, 'background affects ambition and ambition affects both IQ and class values; in addition . . . there is a lesser influence directly from background to class values, directly from background to IQ and directly between IQ and class values.' Elsewhere, he indicates that school rating operates in much the same fashion as (family) background. As for the relationship between the two, (he) notes on the one hand that 'families may choose their place of residence [i.e., the socio-economic status of the school] ,' but also that 'by introducing neighbourhood we may only be measuring family background more precisely'.[26]

We can translate this textual summary of the model accounting for class values into the path diagram in Fig. 8, using vertical lines to indicate points in the time sequence, straight arrowed lines to signify the direction of a causal sequence, and curved, two-headed arrows to show that the causal sequence is not known (as is implied in the last sentence quoted from Duncan). At this stage, we cannot translate the statement that some influences are less powerful than others.

One advantage of path analysis can be seen at once. It is, perhaps, unlikely that the original author would have constructed the model he seems to imply, if he had had to clarify all the connections by drawing a path diagram. In particular, he might have wanted to question the decision that ambition is a partial cause of measured intelligence.

As the diagram stands, it could be arrived at by tabular causal

Fig. 8. CAUSAL MODEL TO ACCOUNT FOR CLASS VALUES IN TERMS OF AMBITION, INTELLIGENCE, FAMILY BACKGROUND AND SCHOOL STATUS

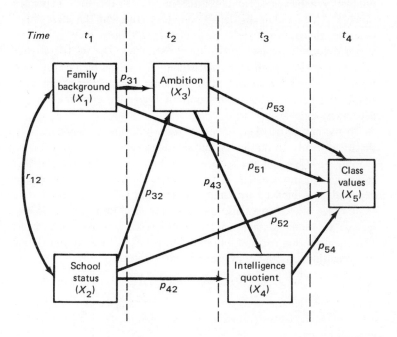

Source. Adapted from Duncan, *op. cit.,* fig. 1, p.4.

analysis, but it would be impossible to specify the relative weights of each arrow. These, the *path coefficients,* are symbolised by *p,* with the first subscript indicating the dependent variable number, and the second the independent variable number. The model is clearly oversimplified as a representation of reality because it depicts a closed system, excluding any other influences other than the four shown. Clearly, we would not expect the diagram to show what influences the earliest variables, X_1 and X_2, whatever kind of analysis was being undertaken, for there would be no stopping the analysis being pushed further and further back in time. But we should perhaps prefer a causal

115

model which indicated the presence of other variables influencing the intervening and dependent variables. In path analysis, additional residual variables are entered into the model for each dependent variable. These unknown, 'error' variables represent the effect of all other variables, unspecified and unmeasured though they be, and are assumed to be unrelated to the known variables. The relative strength of these variables, both independent and 'error', can then be estimated from the correlation matrix of all variables and, in this example, are simply the beta weights in the multiple regression equation for each dependent variable.

To the non-statistician, the use of the word 'simply' may appear as a sleight of hand. An outline of multiple regression was given in the last chapter. It is beyond the scope of this book to explain the statistical techniques in more detail. In the example diagram, ambition (X_3) is depicted as influenced by family background (X_1) and school status (X_2). Since other factors also influence the level of ambition we must include a residual variable (X_r) to take account of all such variables. The equation summarising this situation is not difficult to follow once the weighting subscript convention is understood.

$$X_3 = a_{3.12} + b_{31.2r}X_1 + b_{32.1r}X_2 + b_{3r.12}X_r$$

where b signifies the weighting or relative importance of a variable, and a is a constant factor equivalent to the value of X_3 if X_1, X_2 and X_r were all zero.

The order for subscripts is important. The first subscript refers to the dependent variable, the second to the independent variable, and any subscripts after the dot refer to variables which are held constant. Thus $b_{31.2r}$ means the influence on variable X_3 of variable X_1, *eliminating* the effects of variables X_2 and X_r: the effect of family background on ambition, school status and other things (X_r) being equal.

The numerical values of b will depend upon the units used to measure all the variables. If family background were measured on a three-point scale, the value of $b_{31.2r}$ would be different from its value if it were measured on a 100-point scale; b-weights can only be interpreted in the light, therefore, of all measurement scales in the equation. What they tell us is the amount of direct effect a variable has on another, when the other influential variables do not vary. This is not a measure of an independent variable's *total* effect, since it excludes those indirect effects when, for example, one variable influences another, which in turn influences the dependent variable.

To avoid this problem of the scale of measurement, and also to obtain measures of direct, indirect, and total effects, we need to standardise the *b*-weights, by calculating the multiple regression equation using, not raw scores in the original units, but *standard* scores (each score expressed as a deviation from the mean of that variable, divided by its standard deviation). The weights we now obtain are *beta*-weights in the multiple regression equation, the constant factor *a* disappears, and all weights are comparable, because each measures how much change in the dependent variable, measured in standard deviation units, is brought about by each independent variable. In Duncan's example, the path coefficients are the *beta*-weights.

(This is only true under certain conditions: where the residuals are assumed to be uncorrelated, where there are no other unmeasured variables, and when each potential dependent variable is directly related to all the preceding variables in the causal sequence. When these assumptions cannot be met, a set of simultaneous equations, one for each dependent variable is necessary to calculate path coefficients.)

The causal model with the actual values of the path coefficients is shown in Fig. 9.

This path diagram enables us to give substance to the verbal or qualitative model already described loosely. We can see the relative importance of all four explanatory variables on the index of class values with, for example, school status (0.15) clearly being more significant than home background (0.06). We can also trace the determinants of ambition and intelligence quotient by examining the path coefficients leading to each. Ambition, not normally accorded any place among the social determinants of measured intelligence, here appears to have more influence than either school or home status. The three new arrows leading into ambition, class values, and intelligence measure the combined effect of all variables not taken into account by the model, nor correlated with any of the immediate determinants of the variable to which they point. As well as inducing a suitable level of humility in

117

Fig. 9 PATH DIAGRAM SHOWING PATH COEFFICIENT OBTAINED FROM
EMPIRICAL DATA

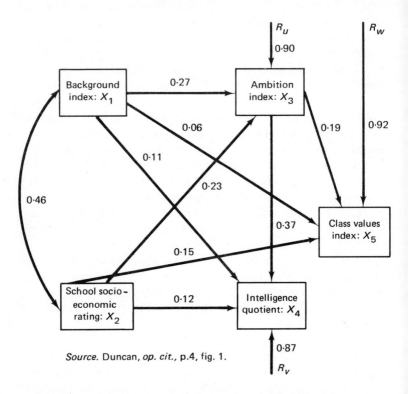

Source. Duncan, *op. cit.,* p.4, fig. 1.

researchers who claim to have explained a dependent variable, they remind us that, *as with all causal explanations,* the results must be interpreted within the context (or model) of all the explanatory variables which have been considered simultaneously. It is simply not true to say that the path coefficient (0.11) from family background to intelligence quotient is *the* effect of family background on measured intelligence, full stop. Ignoring such considerations as sampling variations, the most that can be said is that the path coefficient obtained is the effect in a model which also contains ambition and

118

school status variables. If either variable were excluded, or other significant variables were included, the path coefficient would almost certainly take a new value.

So far, path analysis may appear as no more than a new way of presenting old statistics, these being the *beta* coefficients in a multiple regression equation and the square root of the unexplained variation in a multiple correlation, $\sqrt{(1-R^2)}$, the latter being the residual path coefficient. Where it breaks new ground is in providing a way of separating out the direct and indirect effects of one variable on another, where there is more than one path from the independent to the dependent variable. We can, therefore, specify how one variable influences another. The direct effect of school status on ambition is 0.23, while its indirect effect is 0.12. This is obtained by taking the direct route via family background, and multiplying the effect of family background (0.27) by the correlation between school status and family background (0.46). (The method for obtaining measures of each indirect effects shown here is a special case, not the general method. Duncan's paper does not give the correlation matrix for all five variables which constitutes the data set necessary for showing more generalisable methods. For a clear exposition of path analysis and its basic assumptions and methods, see Land.[27])

Path analysis is based on multiple regression procedures, but its results must be clearly distinguished from those of regression methods. A particular variant of regression often used in this country could easily, and disastrously, be confused with it. In the Plowden Report, Peaker makes a stepwise regression analysis of the data in the national survey, trying to discover what are the most significant variables accounting for primary school children's reading ability.[28] To help readers visualise the results he presents them as a 'path diagram' but, despite apparent similarities, this is not a path analysis. (It should be said, in fairness to Peaker, that his report was written before path analysis had become part of the sociologist's repertoire.)

Stepwise regression
Stepwise regression is essentially an exploratory procedure in attempting to account for an effect variable in terms of a series of

causal variables. Unlike path analysis, in which the analyst constructs his explanatory model and then tests it on his data, in stepwise regression the method itself is responsible for selecting the variables from among all those measured. It qualifies as data dredging of the 'fishing' variety. The procedure picks those variables with least correlation among themselves which, in conjunction with the others, add most to the estimation or prediction of a dependent variable. To understand the differences between path analysis and stepwise regression, it is instructive to examine the Plowden conclusions with those that might have emerged from a path analysis.

It will be remembered that the Plowden research was a random sample survey of the parents of children in primary schools, supplemented by information on the schools themselves. Data on more than one hundred variables were collected which can be divided into those covering parental attitudes, home circumstances, and school variables. The school variables are translated into contextual variables of each pupil.

The 'path diagram' published in the Report suggests the way in which certain home circumstances may cause parental attitudes which in turn may cause reading ability. The contribution of school characteristics is also shown as a cause of reading ability. The measure used for the relative importance of individual determining variables is the proportion of the variance in reading ability accounted for directly by each variable, shown in column 1 of Table 13. We can compare this measure with the figure which a path analysis would produce in columns 2 to 4. The published data only permits us to examine the immediate 'causes' of reading ability, not the earlier parts of the chain by which home circumstances are linked to attitudes.

In the Plowden model, the greatest measured effect is the parent's aspiration for their child, compared with which all other measured effects are much smaller. Each figure shows the proportion of variation in reading ability accounted for when the other measured variables are held constant; 55 per cent of the variation is unaccounted for by the variables considered here.

TABLE 13

A comparison of stepwise regression and path analysis explanations of the same data

Type	Variable	Stepwise regression analysis	Path analysis	
		Prop. of variation in reading ability accounted for	Direct effect on reading ability (DE)	Total indirect effects on reading ability (TIE)
Attitude	Parental aspiration for child	0.29	0.48	0.11
Attitude	Literacy of home	0.06	0.17	0.22
Home circumstance	Physical amenities of home	0.04	0.15	0.13
School	H.M. Inspector's assessment of teacher	0.04	0.16	0.10
School	No. of school functions arranged when fathers available	0.02	0.18	-0.08
Residual	All other (unmeasured) variables	0.55	0.74	

Source. Plowden Report, Vol. 2, table 4.1, p. 209.

Path analysis and stepwise regression compared

With path analysis, the 'direct effect' figures represent the direct influence of an independent on a dependent variable, while the 'total indirect effect' figures provide an estimate of an independent variable's influence on the dependent via all possible indirect routes postulated in the model. Given the intercorrelations of all variables in the model, path analysis would enable us to show the amount of influence in each direct route.

It is evident that the two explanations are totally different. This is because the stepwise regression figures embody both direct (DE) and indirect effects (TIE) for each causal variable, while path analysis has distinguished between the two. Thus, 'parental aspirations for their child' makes its biggest effect directly, while 'literacy of the home' makes its contribution through its effects on other causal variables. The figures for each type of analysis are expressed in different units and so are not directly comparable. The stepwise regression units are proportions of the total 'effect' variance accounted for and are obtained by multiplying the *beta* coefficient by the simple correlation between causal and dependent variables. The path coefficients are proportions of the standard deviation of the dependent variable, with the TIE being the simple correlation minus the path coefficient.

This means that the two residual figures, while they appear different, convey the same information. Because the variance is the standard deviation squared, the residual variance is the square of the residual path coefficient. It should be noted that the size of the residual in path analysis is *not* a measure of the validity of the causal interpretation.[29] It may reflect the inability to include other causal variables in the model, but it does not reflect on the accuracy of the path coefficients obtained. This can be assessed from the standard errors of the *betas*. The internal consistency of the explanatory model is assessed by the extent to which the zero-order correlations between causally linked variables can be reconstructed from the values of the path coefficients.

Properly used, path analysis is a powerful development in explicating causal explanations. By relying upon multiple regression techniques, it avoids many of the inefficiencies and ambiguities we have seen to be inherent in causal analysis through contingency tables. It requires the analyst to consider the implications of the explanation he offers, in terms of the causal relationships among independent variables. It offers a method of quantifying causal influences in a given population and of testing the internal consistency of the model proposed.

Constraints on path analysis

Both the theoretical model and the data must comply with certain requirements.[30] The variables must be capable of being put in a causal order. The earliest variables in the path diagram (school status and family background in Fig. 8) must not be causally related, even if they are correlated. The specification of causal order in the model must be correct; if it is incorrect, the model will fit the data, but its meaning will be a nonsense. The only absolute guide to the correct causal order is the logical statement that a cause must precede its effect. In practice, this guide means that the variables in the model must belong to an undebateable sequence in time; no arrows, single- or double-headed, can be drawn between variables conceivably of the same time period (except double-headed arrows between variables at the starting-point of a model).

A further requirement is what we must assume that all the residual path coefficients are unrelated. In so far as they represent sampling errors of measurement the assumption follows by definition. Residuals, however, represent the aggregate effect of *all* unmeasured variables having an effect on the variable they lead into. If there are many, it seems intrinsically unlikely that all affecting one variable in the model will be unrelated to any unmeasured variables affecting another element in the model. By the same token of their multiplicity, one may perhaps assume that the effects of any correlation between the components of residuals will be swamped or evened out in the aggregate, by the greater influence of genuinely unrelated components.

Finally, all the assumptions necessary for regression analysis are also necessary for path analysis. The cases must have been randomly selected into the study, the variables must have been measured on metric scales or their dummy variable equivalents, and the measurements must be precise and reliable.

Some authors also insist that the variables be linearly related—that is, that a unit increase in one variable is accompanied by the same increase or decrease in the correlated variable at whatever point on either scale it occurs. This assumption rules out the possibility of other types of relatedness between variables, most notably interactive effects. Where an interaction effect is suspected, it can however be transformed into

123

linear terms by expressing the two variables by their logarithmic values (provided, of course, that the model does not contain both transformed and untransformed values of the same variable, which would create artificially related variables). Non-linear relationships have, therefore, to be foreseen; in practice, the assumption of linearity does not seem to be unduly restrictive.

Path analysis is still in its earliest days, and with further development of the method we can confidently expect less restrictive assumptions. The requirement of interval scale measurements for the independent variables has already disappeared in multiple classification analysis, which is essentially a multiple regression procedure with nominal level causal variables. The AID (Automatic Interaction Detector) program is its stepwise analogue.

THE STRATEGY OF SURVEY ANALYSIS

The keynote of the strategy of survey analysis recommended in this volume has been an informed, intelligent, and disciplined appraisal of one's data. Informed, because any data set is likely to contain relationships which appear to support interpretations closer to fantasy than reality. By imaginatively anticipating findings, we are able to test our explanations and understanding of the data at each stage of the analysis, constantly refining or rejecting our ideas as the data requires. With discipline, we are able to set ourselves up as our own devil's advocates, constantly sceptical that our findings are anything but artifacts, devising alternative explanations and deducing critical tests which will eliminate as many as possible of the varying plausible explanations. With intelligence, we can limit our tests and conjectures to realistically plausible alternatives. With these qualities shown in our methods, the analysis will carry more authority with its readership.

But no work of science can conclude with an appeal to authority. The final arbiter must be the empirically collected evidence. If the findings seem important, they need to be replicated first on comparable samples, and secondly on samples for which different factors might be expected to modify the results. The first replication can best be achieved, if the sample size allows, by setting aside before analysis begins, a random sample of the data. The data can then be intelligently explored or even dredged in the first subsample, and the results tested on the second, replication subsample. If they hold up substantially, or if splitting the sample is impractical, it may be possible to attempt to replicate the findings on survey data collected elsewhere and for other purposes. With the advent of data banks, such as the S.S.R.C. Survey Archive at Essex University, secondary analysis of this replication kind is becoming increasingly possible. The results may not support one's primary findings or, more fruitfully, they may help to specify the kinds of conditions in which they hold good.

CHESTER COLLEGE LIBRARY

References and further reading

CHAPTER 1. THE NATURE OF SURVEY ANALYSIS

1. P.F. Lazarsfeld, 'Evidence and inference in social research', *Daedalus,* 87, no. 4 (1958), 109.
2. T. Hirschi and H. Selvin, *Delinquency Research: an appraisal of analytic methods,* N.Y. Free Press, 1967, p. 11.
3. *Ibid.,* p. 12.
4. The survey is fictitious, but the diet is real. See, for example, Elizabeth Marshall-Thomas, *Warrior Herdsmen,* Knopf 1965. The people are the Karamojong of north-eastern Uganda.
5. G. Sjoberg and R. Nett, *A Methodology for Social Research,* Harper & Row, 1968, p. 263.
6. M. Young and P. Willmott, *Family and Kinship in East London,* Routledge, 1957; J.A. Platt, *Social Research in Bethnal Green,* Macmillan, 1971.
7. Platt., p. 52
8. *Ibid.,* p. 51.
9. W.E. Deming, 'On errors in surveys', *American Sociological Review,* 19, (1944), 359–69.
10. Quoted by C.A. Moser, *Survey Methods in Social Investigation,* Humanities Press, 1958, p. 19.
11. G.U. Yule, 'An investigation into the causes of changes in pauperism in England, *Journal of the Royal Statistical Society,* 62 (1899), 249–86.
12. C.Y. Glock, (ed.), *Survey Research in the Social Sciences,* N.Y., Russell Sage, 1967, p. xvi.

CHAPTER 2. CLASSIFYING, MEASURING AND CODING

1. T.B. Bottomore and M. Rubel, *Karl Marx, Selected Writings in Sociology and Social Philosophy,* 2nd edn, (1963), Penguin Books, pp. 210–12.
2. An example of a data matrix is a teacher's mark-sheets on which each pupil's name is listed vertically, the subjects taught are listed horizontally, and a mark for every subject for every pupil is entered in the appropriate cell created by the rows and columns.
3. Analysts are of course more concerned with substantive meaning in their data then with techniques of analysis. There are no substantive advantages in breaking down a nominal variable into alternative attributes: the advantages are to statisticians for whom binomial statistics are better understood than multinomial statistics, and to computer programmers who work with machines which reduce all data to binary form anyway.
4. Royal College of Physicians, *Smoking and Health* (1962), table IV.1, p. 44.
5. It will not escape the knowledgeable observer that this table is a perfect example of a Guttman scale (of measurement level).
6. Two statistical textbooks which adopt this approach and, incidentally, are excellent in their own right, are H.M. Blalock, *Social Statistics,* 2nd edn., McGraw-Hill, 1972; and S. Siegel, *Nonparametric Statistics for the Behavioural Sciences,* McGraw-Hill, 1956.
7. By J.A. Davis in an excellent and readable first chapter to his *Elementary Survey Analysis,* Prentice-Hall, 1971.
8. These criteria are based upon P.F. Lazarsfeld and A.H. Barton, 'Qualitive measurements in the social sciences: classification, typologies, and indices', in D. Lerner and H. Lasswell, eds., *The Policy Sciences,* Stanford University Press, 1951, pp. 155–92.
9. *Ibid.,* p. 158.
10. *Ibid.,* p. 167.
11. J. Silvey, 'The occupational attitudes of secondary school leavers in Uganda', in R. Jolly, ed., *Education in Africa,* East African Publishing House, 1969.
12. Central Advisory Council for Education, *Children and their*

Primary Schools (Plowden Report), H.M.S.O. 1967, Vol. 2, App. 3: The 1964 National Survey among Parents of Primary School Children, pp. 166 and 142.

13. S.M. Lipset, M. Trow and J.S. Coleman, *Union Democracy,* N.Y., Free Press, 1956.

14. M. Stacey, ed., *Comparability in Social Research,* Heinemann, 1969.

15. The tension between the two approaches is stimulating and tantalisingly dealt with throughout G. Sjoberg and R. Nett, *A Methodology for Social Research,* Harper & Row, 1968.

16. Lazarsfeld and Barton, pp. 166–7.

17. *Ibid.,* p. 160.

18. C. Kadushin, 'Individual decisions to undertake psychotherapy', *Administrative Science Quarterly,* 3, 1959, 379–411.

19. *Ibid.,* p. 379.

20. H. Zeisel, *Say It With Figures,* 5th edn, Harper & Row, 1968, ch. 10. esp. p. 131.

21. Plowden Report, p. 97.

22. George Gallup, *Qualitative Measurement of Public Opinion: The Quintamensional Plan of Question Design,* 1947.

23. J. Roth, 'Hired hand research', *American Sociologist,* 1, 1966, pp. 190–6.

24. C.A. Moser, *Survey Methods in Social Investigations,* Humanities Press, 1958, p. 280.

25. P. Lazarsfeld, 'Reflections on business', *American Journal of Sociology,* 65, no. 1 (1959), 4.

26. As good a starting point as any for discussions of reliability and validity is C. Seltiz *et al.,* 1962, *Research Methods in Social Relations,* especially ch. 5, Methuen.

27. M. Rosenberg, *Society and the Adolescent Self-Image,* Princeton University Press (1965), p. 31.

28. Hirschi and Selvin, *Delinquency Research,* p. 211.

CHAPTER 3 PRODUCING TABLES

1. Plowden Report, Vol. 2, p. 102.

2. *Ibid.,* p. 100.
3. E. Durkheim, *Suicide,* Routledge, 1952, p. 39.
4. W. Rodgers, *Think,* London, Granada, 1971, p. 77.
5. Quoted by J.P. Mandeville, 'Improvements in methods of census and surveys', *Journal of the Royal Statistical Society,* 109. (1946), 111–29.
6. D.T. Muxworthy, 'A survey program for the mid-seventies' (mimeograph), Edinburgh Regional Computing Centre, 1973.
7. H.H. Nie, D.H. Bent and C.H. Hull, *Statistical Package for the Social Sciences,* McGraw-Hill, 1970.

CHAPTER 4 DECIPHERING THE MEANING OF VARIABLES

1. For example J. Cook-Gumperz, *Social Control and Socialisation,* Routledge, 1973, p. 59.
2. This discussion owes much to Hirschi and Selvin, *Delinquency Research,* pp. 210–11.
3. *The Classification of Occupations,* 1970 outlines the current system in use. Its origins are outlined by T.A.C. Stevenson in 'The vital statistics of wealth and poverty', *Journal of the Royal Statistical Society,* 91 (128), 207–30.
4. J. Hall and D. Caradog Jones, 'Social grading of occupations', *British Journal of Sociology,* 1 (1950), 31–55.
5. P.M. Blau and O.D. Duncan, *The American Occupational Structure,* Wiley, 1967, pp. 118–23.
6. L.J. Newson and E.A. Newson, *Four Years Old in an Urban Community,* Allen & Unwin: Penguin, 1968.
7. Stevenson, p. 212.
8. J.W.D. Douglas, *The Home and the School,* Humanities Press, 1968.
9. A.B. Hollingshead and F.C. Redlich, *Social Class and Mental Illness,* Wiley, 1958 (Appendix 2).
10. *Ibid.,* p. 395.
11. *Ibid.,* p. 397.
12. W. Brandis and D. Henderson, *Social Class, Language and Communication,* Routledge, 1970, Appendix I, 130–6.

13. Plowden Report, pp. 145 and 151.
14. D. Child, *Essential of Factor Analysis* (Holt, Rinehart & Winston, 1970), is a useful introduction. H.H. Harman, *Modern Factor Analysis* (University of Chicago Press, 1968), is a comprehensive, standard text.
15. *Office of Population Censuses and Surveys,* H.M.S.O., 1973, pp. 188–93.

CHAPTER 5 PATHWAYS THROUGH DATA

1. *General Household Survey,* p. 80, Office of Population Censuses and Surveys, H.M.S.O., 1973.
2. M. Trow, 'Survey research and education', in Glock, ed., *Survey Research in the Social Sciences* (1967), p. 367.
3. Bunge, M. quoted by H.M. Blalock, 1961, *Causal Inferences in Non-Experimental Research,* University of N. Carolina Press, 1961, p. 6.
4. W.G. Cochran, F. Mosteller and J.W. Tukey, quoted by Hirschi and Selvin, *Delinquency Research,* pp. 94–5.
5. Trow, p. 368.
6. *General Household Survey,* p. 95.
7. Glock, for example, in Survey Research, p. 28.
8. Quoted by M. Rosenberg, 1968, *The Logic of Survey Analysis,* pp. 88–89.
9. H.C. Selvin, 'Durkheim's *Suicide* and Problems of Empirical Research', *American Journal of Sociology,* 63, 1958, 608.
10. Durkheim, *Suicide,* Table XXI, p. 178.
11. *Ibid.,* p. 184.
12. *Ibid.,* p. 186–7.
13. Herbert Hyman, *Survey Design and Analysis,* N.Y., Free Press, 1955, p. 308.
14. J.A. Davis, 'Compositional effects, role systems, and the survival of small discussion groups', *Public Opinion Quarterly,* 25, 1961, 575.
15. Two useful clarifications of contextual analysis by Lazarsfeld and Kendall, and Coleman can be found in A. Etzioni, ed., *A Sociological Reader on Complex Organisations,* 2nd edn, Holt Reinhardt & Winston, 1970, pp. 499–527.

16. Rosenberg, pp. 99–100.
17. Hirschi and Selvin, *Delinquency Research,* pp. 166–7.
18. *Ibid.,* p. 164.
19. See the readings in D.E. Morrison and R.E. Henkel, 1970, *The Significance Test Controversy.*
20. H.C. Selvin and A. Stuart, 'Data dredging procedures in survey analysis', *American Statistician,* June 1966, pp. 20–3.
21. *Ibid.,* p. 22.
22. J.N. Morgan and J.A. Sonquist, 'Problems in the Analysis of Survey Data and a Proposal', *Journal of the American Statistical Association,* 58, 1963, p. 231.
23. C. Jencks, *et al., Inequality,* 1973, p. 226 and p. 346.
24. J. Fennesey, 'Some problems and possibilities in policy related research', *Social Science Research,* 1, 1972, 4.
25. O.D. Duncan, 1966, 'Path analysis: sociological examples', *American Journal of Sociology,* 72, no. 1, 1966, 1–16.
26. *Ibid.,* pp. 3-4.
27. K.C. Land, 'Principles of path analysis', *Sociological Methodology,* 1969, pp. 3–37.
28. Plowden Report, Vol. 2, pp. 186 and 209.
29. P.M. Blau and O.D. Duncan, *The American Occupational Structure,* Wiley, 1967, p. 175.
30. D.R. Heise, 'Problems in path analysis and causal inferences', *Sociological Methodology,* 1969, pp. 38–73.

Index